. . . They had to carry him to the hospital. He couldn't walk because every step caused unbearable pain. He was an arthritic, far advanced.

The doctors questioned him routinely. Had he been working the past year? Yes, he had been driving a bulldozer until a few days before.

"Driving a bulldozer! How were you able to do that?"

He told them he had devised ways of pushing the levers with his wrists and arms instead of his hands. He worked the foot controls with his heels instead of his toes. To put in oil or water he had to cradle the can in his arms. He couldn't even climb into the seat himself; his friends had to lift him.

"But why did you keep on working in such a condition?" they asked in amazement.

He smiled. "I have a wife and four children," he said simply.

His feet were so bad that surgery had to be performed on them. Afterwards he was given a full program of treatment.

Three months later he was ready to work again.

It has been written into the record of this man's treatment that his own overwhelming desire to recover should get credit for at least half the victory. The same unstoppable will that kept him driving a bulldozer long after his physical condition had collapsed was the thing that enabled him to overcome the arthritis itself. He overcame arthritis because he would not give in.

If you will supply the desire to recover—the faith that you can recover—this book will supply the physical therapy procedures, to be carried on at home with the help of a friend, through which you will be able to overcome your arthritis.

OVERCOME

ARTHRITIS

by WILLIAM KITAY

formerly Science and Medical Editor,

Arthritis & Rheumatism Foundation

GRAMERCY PUBLISHING COMPANY

NEW YORK

To
FLOYD B. ODLUM
*whose own suffering from the terrible disease
created a kinship with some 11 million Americans
similarly afflicted and whose love and concern
for his fellow man led him to found
The Arthritis And Rheumatism Foundation*

*This edition published by Gramercy Publishing Co.,
a division of Crown Publishers, Inc., by
arrangement with Prentice-Hall, Inc.*
l m n o p

SOME WORDS
OF THANKS...

THE DEMAND FOR A MEDICALLY ACCURATE AND COMPLETE
handbook for arthritis sufferers has been growing for several
years. No book previously published answers this demand.

The Arthritis and Rheumatism Foundation has received many
letters from general practitioners, medical school professors, and
arthritis specialists suggesting—urging—that a book be written
that would accurately and honestly tell the story of arthritis.
More than that, they wanted a book that would clearly picture
the all-important role that the arthritic has in his own treatment.

Letters also came from the 45 local Chapters of the Foundation, saying that the people to whom they owe a great responsibility, their home-town supporters, were demanding such a
book.

It is to answer those demands—to fill a very definite need in
the fight to overcome arthritis—that I have written this book.

During my five exciting years as Science Editor of the Arthritis
and Rheumatism Foundation and the American Rheumatism
Association, I was privileged to associate with the country's fore-
most arthritis specialists, chief among whom were Doctors
Ronald W. Lamont-Havers, the Associate Medical Director of
the Foundation, and Doctor Russell L. Cecil, the Medical Director. To these two men, in connection with the writing of this
book, I owe a large debt.

I also wish to express my gratitude to the many arthritis
specialists throughout the nation whose work, whose writings,
whose lectures and whose many personal discussions with me

helped make this book possible. They are:

Dr. Hans Waine, Boston, Medical Director of the New England Chapter of the Arthritis and Rheumatism Foundation.

Dr. Gideon K. de Forest, Head of the Arthritis Clinic at the Yale University School of Medicine.

Dr. Richard H. Freyberg, Director of the Arthritis Clinic at New York's Hospital for Special Surgery and Chairman of the Medical and Scientific Committee of The Foundation.

Dr. Currier McEwen, head of the Arthritis Study Group at the New York University Medical School.

Dr. Charles Ragan, Chief of the Arthritis Clinic at New York's Columbia Presbyterian Hospital.

Dr. Ralph H. Boots, Director of the Arthritis Clinic at Columbia Presbyterian Hospital.

Dr. Edward W. Lowman, Clinical Director of the Institute for Physical Medicine and Rehabilitation.

Dr. Norman O. Rothermich, Columbus, Ohio, Medical Director, Ohio Chapter, Arthritis and Rheumatism Foundation.

Dr. Edward Boland, Los Angeles, California.

Dr. Robert M. Stecher, Cleveland, Ohio, Medical Director, Cleveland Chapter, Arthritis and Rheumatism Foundation and President, La League Internationale Contre Le Rheumatisme.

Dr. Otto Steinbrocker, New York, Chief of the Arthritis Clinics at Lenox Hill Hospital and the Hospital for Joint Diseases.

Also, my sincere thanks to John E. Walsh, editor, Prentice-Hall, Inc., who worked so hard and so skillfully to prepare the manuscript for publication.

Finally, words cannot express my appreciation to my wife, Ida, for her encouragement, her patience, and her valuable editorial assistance. And to my son, Calvin and my daughter, Cynthia, for being so grown-up in letting their daddy alone during the writing of the book.

WILLIAM KITAY

CONTENTS

PART 2 • •

WHAT YOU SHOULD KNOW
ABOUT ARTHRITIS

INTRODUCTION

by Hans Selye, M. D.

OVER THE YEARS, IN THE RESEARCH I HAVE CONDUCTED ON stress and its effect on the human body, I have had a close and interested relationship both with arthritis sufferers and with the physicians to whom they turn for help. One thing this association has taught me is an appreciation for the problems that challenge my clinical colleagues.

Perhaps the greatest problem the physician today has in combatting arthritis and the rheumatic diseases is the misinformation that exists about these ailments. The many quack cures and the old-wives tales that have grown up around the arthritis sufferer demonstrate the need for an accurate telling of the arthritis story.

Here, in this book, the reader will not only find an accurate and honest accounting of arthritis and the various forms that it takes, but he will also find useful and helpful information that will aid him immeasurably in his fight against these widespread and often crippling diseases.

As important as is the story about arthritis, so is the arthritis patient's ability to use this information. Most doctors in the field strongly feel that a patient should be able to augment the efforts of his doctor by continuing certain forms of physical therapy at home. It has been found that selected exercises and the use of heat, for example, can effectively prevent or minimize the misery and the crippling associated with the disease. However, to be effective, these techniques must be used regularly and repeatedly. The home is the only logical, as it is the most economical, place for such a program of constant care.

Toward this aim, readers will find the section on Home Care useful and helpful. The various techniques of Home Care given here are not meant to replace professional medical care, nor should they be used in this way. Home Care is intended to supplement and extend your doctor's efforts. Properly used under the direction and supervision of your doctor, Home Care can prove highly effective.

This book is based on a simple premise. It is that there is hope for every arthritis sufferer, no matter how severe his disease may be. Aided by early diagnosis, numerous techniques are now available that can diminish the activity of the disease and lessen the damage it may cause. Even the severest of cases, no matter how complicated, can be reclaimed and restored to a useful and productive life.

True, there is no one treatment for all persons with arthritis. Neither is arthritis a single and a specific disease. Nor are all aches and pains due to arthritis. Arthritis doctors believe that the person with arthritis should not be a passive recipient of therapy. They say that if he is to make any progress against the disease, if he is to recover, he must join with his doctor as an active participant in a prescribed program of treatment.

To work with his doctor intelligently, the arthritis patient should have a good general understanding about his disease. He must have honest and truthful information. He must know what his doctor is trying to do for him and he must appreciate his doctor's limitations.

The arthritis patient must also have some idea of the approach that his doctor is taking in trying to manage his problem and suppress the effects of the disease. He must realize the limits of the various drugs and the other forms of therapy being used. He must also have some realization of his chances of recovery and of the degree in which he will be returned to a useful, independent and productive life.

It is in this respect that this book fulfills a great need. Your doctor would like nothing better than to be able to sit down and spend an hour or two with you explaining the problem of arthritis and how it affects you and the challenging task that lies ahead in your case.

In one large well-known clinic in the United States, this is done through regular classes held for arthritis patients. Persons being cared for at this clinic attend a series of lectures where they learn about their disease and about what their doctors are trying to do for them. They are taught that their cooperation is essential to their recovery and they are also shown just how they can cooperate with their doctors.

It would certainly be ideal if all arthritics could attend a series of such lectures. Perhaps, some day, a mass educational effort of this kind will be available. It would be still more desirable if every doctor could take the time to explain to each arthritis patient all that the patient should know. This, of course, is physically impossible.

To tell even the outlines of the arthritis story to just one patient would take even the most articulate doctor more than an hour. The demand upon his services being what it is, no doctor is able to take this time from his practice. Most doctors in the field of arthritis have far more than they can possibly do, dividing their time between private practice and the arthritis clinics in their communities.

For a long time, doctors working with arthritics have felt a need for a book they can confidently recommend to their patients that would accurately detail the arthritis story. To be useful, such a book would also have to be able to guide and instruct the person with arthritis in how he can effect a closer working relationship with his doctor.

This book, it seems to me, fills that need. It is a book that every arthritis sufferer should read and study and use. It is a book that should be in every home where there is arthritis, for the information that it contains and the lessons that it imparts can be of great assistance in your efforts to combat the disease.

William Kitay, the author, is a science writer, a reporter who has covered the field of health and medicine for more than ten years. His articles on arthritis and on other health subjects have appeared in newspapers and leading magazines. He has also written a book on bursitis. In *Overcome Arthritis* he describes the current medical practice followed by doctors who specialize in this field, and tells you in a clear and easy-to-read style the progress of the research scientists who are engaged in a concerted effort to learn more about arthritis and perhaps even identify the basic cause of this group of diseases.

Throughout the book, and in an interesting closing chapter that lists 101 of the most common questions asked today about arthritis, you will find the answers to most everything you have been asking about this disease.

Carefully read and judiciously used in cooperation with your physician, this book may well be a turning point in your fight against the painful, distressing, and devastating effects of arthritis.

Montreal, Que.

YOU NEED NOT SUFFER
ARTHRITIC PAIN AND
DISABILITY ANY LONGER

Arthritics live in a world of pain, helplessness, and confusion

WHEN ARTHRITIS STRIKES, WITH ALL ITS PAIN, SWELLING, and stiffness, there follow closely the demons of worry and fear. As the pain gets worse, the worry grows; and as the stiffness begins to interfere with normal living, nagging fright becomes a daily companion.

When the unfortunate sufferer tries to find a way out, he finds only the confusion of claims and counterclaims. What

1

is worse, he is sometimes told that there is nothing that can be done, that there is no cure for him.

How much worry and pain and helplessness have you put up with in the past year?

Unless you're a lot different from most other arthritics, you've had your share of misery during the last twelve months not even counting the years before that.

And there probably is no need to tell you of the confusion, ignorance, and general air of hopelessness that surround arthritis and its treatment.

How many times have you had to do your work with arthritic pain stealing your energy and dulling your efforts? How many times have you looked with a sinking heart at swollen joints and twisted fingers? How many times have the tears almost gathered to your eyes when you thought how dependent you were on the kindness of other people?

I know your answer: too many! Too many!

These thoughts, these cries for help could be yours

Letters poured into the Arthritis Foundation for which I was Science Editor. It was my job to answer them. The sad cry was always the same: *Is there any help for us?*

Maybe you never wrote a letter asking for help. But weren't these people putting your thoughts into words:

. . . have taken many medicines . . . read articles . . . am competely confused . . . broken financially, mentally and physically . . .

. . . unable to obtain definite information locally . . .

. . . won't you take me and experiment on me . . .

. . . have a feeling that the disease is spreading slowly . . .

The simple truth is that arthritis can be successfully treated

It's not too hard to understand why there is confusion about arthritis. *But there shouldn't be any confusion;* at least not any more.

For techniques are now available that can calm the pains and activity of arthritis and lessen the damage it may cause. Even the severest of cases, no matter how complicated, can be reclaimed and restored to a useful life.

You help to cure yourself—and you do it at home

Until only a few years ago doctors knew no more about how to treat arthritis than healers had known for thousands of years before. No doctor could give any better advice than: "go home, keep warm, and take it easy."

Today that same advice, with a significant addition, can be used as the starting point on your road to recovery.

And that addition is the Home Care Program given to you in this book; a five-point program that can mean painless, useful living for you.

Relative, friend—anyone—can be your "specialist"

The Home Care Program in this book is *scientific physical therapy adapted for daily use in the home*. But it requires no expensive gadgets with flashing lights and whirling dials. And the highly specialized skills of a highly paid therapist are not necessary.

Anyone who is willing to help you can learn the simple techniques involved. And detailed instructions are given for making the apparatus you will need, at little or no cost.

You can overcome arthritic misery if you really want to

For five years a famous hospital studied the problem of arthritis. In its final report it said: "*The person with arthritis who . . . understands what his doctors are trying to do for him . . . and who has learned how to help his doctors help him in his recovery, is the person who will respond to therapy and who will recover.*"

It even went so far as to say that the person who cannot cooperate intelligently with his doctor is a poor risk, and should not be accepted for treatment.

You can be an intelligent teammate of your doctor

The best way to understand what your doctor is trying to do for you is to know as much as possible about arthritis; and to know the truth about it.

You should know: what arthritis is, what is known of its causes, the different forms it takes and the special treatments involved, why medicine no longer looks to the "wonder" drugs for miracle cures.

You should know that there is no such thing as a special diet for arthritics. A well-rounded diet is essential to good general health, and your body's resistance to any kind of disease is strengthened when your health is good. But aside from the question of *weight-reducing* or *weight-increasing*, diets play no part in the treatment of arthritis.

Learn how to recognize quack cures—and avoid them

Diet isn't the only field in which arthritis quackery operates. Some unfortunate arthritics have actually been persuaded to sit in uranium mines, or to sleep with uranium rocks under their pillows. If you're going to work intelligently with your doctor, you have to understand this problem of quack cures and phony remedies.

The more you know about what *isn't* true, the more you will understand about what *is* true.

In the Home Care Program you help your doctor to help you

When the old-fashioned doctor told his arthritic patients to go home, keep warm, and take it easy, he was on the right track. He just didn't go far enough. For it is in your own home that you can supply the most important elements in the treatment of your arthritis.

That doctor told his patients to keep warm; he knew there was curative power in *heat*. But it has to be correctly applied. So in this book's Home Care Program *you are told how to get the benefits of heat in eleven different ways*.

That doctor told his patients to take it easy; he knew there was curative power in *rest*. But resting, too, has to be done correctly. So, in this book's Home Care Program you will find out that *resting is not just lying down or slouching in an armchair*. There are definite techniques you can apply. They are simple techniques but based on scientific fact.

Good posture, massage, and special exercise are part of your home care program, too

That old-time doctor knew there was something in heat and rest, but he had no conception of the good that may be obtained from *correct posture*; how it can ease pain, lessen fatigue, and reduce the chances of crippling.

Probably the most important parts of your Home Care Program are the two remaining points: *massage*, and *special exercises*.

The methods for treating arthritis in this book have proved successful time and again

The work and knowledge of more than *one thousand* arthritis specialists and research scientists have been put between the covers of this book. That vast pool of knowledge has resulted not only in the *five-point program for daily home care*, but a complete presentation of all available information on arthritis.

In effect, that huge group of scientists has been working for you, searching for a way to help you conquer the pain and disability of arthritis.

At this very moment you hold in your hands the result of the greatest mass attack on the problem of arthritis ever undertaken

An all-out attack on the problem of arthritis was undertaken only with the founding of the Arthritis and Rheumatism Foundation. It drew to the ranks of good health the needed knowledge, money, time, and unselfish effort. The mystery of arthritic suffering had never before been tracked down by such an intensive, organized "detective" force.

The experience of that Foundation has become the basis of this book.

To repeat, science says you can recover from arthritis

The findings of that five-year research study already mentioned cannot be repeated too often. It is the key to the doorway to normal living for you. It is the lever with which you can begin to remove the dead weight of arthritic misery from your body. It can give you the buoyant, pain-free living that *should* be yours.

Here, in effect, is what it said:

If you want to recover from arthritis, there are two things you must do. You must understand what arthritis is all about, and you must learn how to cooperate in the treatment you receive. Do this and you will overcome arthritis.

With the help of this book you can fulfill both requirements. In other words, this book is a *vital* part of your treatment.

Would you change your way of looking at life to recover from arthritis?

"What a question!" you say. Of course you would!

But it is precisely the *mental attitude* of some arthritics that prevents them from returning to independent, normal living. Bogged down by worry, exhausted by fright-thoughts, clouded in ignorance of the disease, thrashing in the quicksand of quackery and superstition, it is little wonder that hopeless resignation creeps into the mind of the arthritic.

Emotions are a part of the pattern of arthritic disease, so *hope* becomes part of your treatment, too.

Throw off despondency, put on optimism

Nothing is surer than this: among the many methods of treatment that are at last available, there is some combination that is best for you. And a great part—I could even say the most important part—of the treatment you can do in your own home.

Isn't that reason enough to be optimistic? Isn't that reason enough to let your heart catch the fire of hope?

Don't take things so hard; *remember, you can recover!* Smile in the face of pain and disability. That's right, *smile;* for now you know that soon pain and disability will be gone from your life.

All right, you say, you're convinced. So what's the next step?

As soon as your doctor has diagnosed your complaint as arthritis and has started treatment, you can start making use of the Home Care Program in this book. Consult with him to find out which parts of the program will be best for you, for the particular form your arthritis has taken.

Select someone, friend or relative, to act as your assistant, and you're on your way to recovery.

Home care is the most practical and effective means of treating arthritis

A daily program of home care will do more for you than you probably realize. Along with presenting you with a simplified schedule of therapy, it has an immense psychological value in *giving you the most important part to play in the treatment of your disease.*

It puts an end to aimless wishing, and it bolsters your hope with positive action.

It permits *daily repetition* of therapy, so that the good you gain today is not lost by tomorrow.

It involves little or no expense, which in itself does away with one of the main causes of arthritic worry.

Watch for that first sign of improvement

The things that will determine how long you must continue with your Home Care Program are: the kind of arthritis you have, how long you have had it and how severe it is, and how faithfully you follow directions.

But sooner or later you will see the first joyous sign of improvement. It might be a lessening of pain, a longer time between attacks, reducing of a swelling, greater and more pain-free use of the joints.

But whatever it is you will see it, you will feel it. And that first sign of improvement will be the greatest single step toward full recovery. Why?

The answer is obvious; you probably have thought of it already. That first sign will be *indisputable proof* that you have arrested your arthritis and started your body on the way to normal, pain-free, independent living.

Part One contains your Home Care Program

Even though the chapters detailing the Home Care Program are written in a simple, easy-to-follow way, I have thought it best to make sure you get off to a good start by having a little discussion on exactly what Home Care is and how it will help you. This you will find in the first chapter.

Then the next seven chapters contain the details. Remember what the five points were? *Rest, Good Posture, Heat, Mas-*

sage, and *Exercise.* Let's give each of these elements a quick look.

Rest will lessen pain, and strengthen your body's natural powers

Rest will do a lot to overcome arthritic pain and disability, but *you have to know how to rest.* When medical science talks about rest it means *complete body rest,* with the whole body or just the involved joints immobilized in just the correct manner.

Maybe you didn't know that the height of your chair or the firmness of your mattress makes a difference. It does, and that's one of the resting techniques explained for you in the chapter on Rest.

Correct posture gets rid of unnatural tensions and stores up energy

When your body is not "stacked" correctly, unnatural tensions are built up; the laws of body mechanics are violated. These things aggravate your arthritic pains, and sap your energy. *Discouragement* goes hand-in-hand with pain and exhaustion, not to mention unnecessary worry and exaggerated fears.

The techniques you will need to achieve and maintain good posture are all in Chapter 3.

Heat correctly applied calms aches and pains

The disabilities of arthritis are bad enough, but it's the pain that causes the real suffering.

Relieve the pains and you will be in a more receptive frame of mind for the other forms of therapy in your Home Care Program. And your arthritic joints will be better able to tolerate the massages and special exercises.

Chapter 4 opens the door for you to the magic of pain-relief through heat.

Massage will do many things for you

Massage is not a haphazard thing, it is a medical art. But it is an art that can be learned by any normally intelligent person, when he is once shown how.

Massage, like heat, will relieve aches, pains, soreness, and muscle spasm.

But it will also increase the circulation within an arthritic joint, thereby providing a more constant supply of fresh blood. And it reduces swelling by speeding the drainage of waste matter from the joint.

What is more it helps the bodily substance called "lymph" to carry off a certain pain-causing chemical about which little is known.

And it has a kind of sedative effect that will give blessed relaxation to your distraught body.

Simple and clear instructions for the use of massage are given in Chapter 5.

You must learn how to exercise correctly

There is a popular misconception among arthritics. They think they must keep moving if they are to prevent joints from becoming stiff and useless. So the idea of motion is in their minds. Any kind of motion.

But all that *undirected* and casual motion will do is exhaust your bodily powers of resistance.

Are you one of the people who has the wrong idea about exercise? If you are then Chapter 6 will be very important for you.

True arthritic exercise is a combination of carefully designed scientific procedures intended to carry an affected joint through its normal range of motion. Each exercise is aimed at overcoming a very definite problem in a particular joint.

The best thing of all

As your attitude towards yourself and your disease improves, the progress you will make in your Home Care Program will step up in tempo. Regardless of the inroads the disease may have made, it will matter little to you and will hardly interfere with your usefulness as an individual.

Best of all, you will be assisting your own recovery, in your own home, and with the help of family and friends.

Full answers to your questions about arthritis are in Part Two

An arthritic who knows nothing about arthritis doesn't make a very good patient, and it's the good patient—the informed patient—who stands the best chance of overcoming the pains and disabilities of arthritis.

The second part of this book is your layman's encyclopedia of arthritic knowledge, in the kind of language that the non-medical man can understand.

You will find chapters with such titles as: "Don't Fall for Special Diets or Quack Cures," "Here's the Whole Truth About Drugs," "Quick Answers to 101 Basic Questions."

Every chapter has a short summary

After each chapter you will find short notes that summarize the chapter for you. These will help you to keep the main points constantly in mind, or will serve as a quick reference.

The more you can remember—that is make a part of your daily thinking—about arthritis, the better you will perform your Home Care therapy. You will be a better patient and a more self-assured person.

But you can't be expected to remember everything you read in this book at first. So these short summaries will do your "remembering" for you.

Begin now—pain-free living can be yours

You know now there is a way of life that can not only prevent recurring attacks of the disease, but can even overcome the pains and disability of arthritis entirely. Begin now to put it into practice.

Turn to the Home Care Program. Browse through it. Get an idea what it's all about. Become familiar with it, as you would be familiar with a friend.

For this Program—this book—can be the best friend that you, as an arthritic, have ever had.

(pages 16-18 combined on this page)

PART 1

WHAT YOU CAN DO TO OVERCOME ARTHRITIS AT HOME

Through faithful use of this Home Care Program it is possible to:

STOP THE PAIN
GET BACK ON YOUR FEET
RETURN TO USEFUL LIVING

~~ 1

WHAT HOME CARE IS
AND HOW IT HELPS YOU

HOME CARE IS A "DO IT YOURSELF" PROGRAM IN WHICH you will actively join with your physician to assure and complete your recovery. Once you start on home care, it will be you and not your physician who will be stopping the pain, preventing crippling, and speeding the return of full motion to your arthritic joints.

But home care is by no means intended to replace whatever other treatment he has prescribed for you. Most likely, you will have to continue with some form of medication, usually aspirin, to ease the distress of the disease, thus permitting you to use the physical therapy procedures that are the basis of home care.

Eases the drain on your pocketbook

Rest is basic to your recovery. Next to a stay in a hospital, sufficient rest can only be obtained in the home. It is in your home too that *heat, massage, and exercise can be effectively administered without the need for elaborate or expensive gadgets or even incurring the continued expense of a professional therapist.*

"If sufficiently detailed outlines are given, a large number of arthritic patients are able to continue treatments at home. Home care is cheaper than hospitalization," Dr. Morris A. Bowie, Director of the Arthritis Clinic at Bryn Mawr Hospital, said in sounding the idea of home care.

Many of the tools and pieces of equipment you will need are readily available to you in your home. A floor lamp can easily and quickly be converted into an infrared heat lamp. An old treadle sewing machine may make a useful foot exerciser. Should there be anything special that you will need, chances are you will be able to build it yourself or have someone build it for you at little cost. (*In later chapters you will find detailed instructions for building everything from a therapeutic baker to a whirlpool bath jet.*) As far as hiring a therapist is concerned, you already have one in your home in the person of a member of your family, whom your doctor or a professional therapist will be able to instruct in the modes of physical therapy prescribed for you.

Permits the basic element: repetition

More important still is that home care will permit you to employ the *one basic element* essential to every successful program of physical therapy, *repetition*. The immediate effects of rest, heat, massage and exercise are short-lived. The good these measures can do must be patiently and deliberately built up over a period of time. Dr. James J. Lightbody, head of an arthritis clinic in Michigan, stated that "physical therapy will do very little good unless applied frequently and also applied only to those who are making an effort to help themselves."

If you are to make any progress at all against the inroads

of arthritis, it will be necessary for you to rest several hours a day. It will also be necessary for you to apply heat and to have your involved joints massaged and exercised a number of times every day.

This repetition that is so necessary can only be obtained in home care. You cannot be expected to make several visits a day to a physiotherapist. Calling a physical therapist into your home will not provide the answer either. Not only is there a dire shortage of these valuable medical aides but even if you were able to retain one, the cost of having one come into your home several times a day or even once every day would certainly be prohibitive.

Home care brings you into the picture

So, you can readily see how important home care can be. It offers you the effective and essential means of easing the miseries of arthritis and of staving off the destructive effects of the disease. Home care also brings you into the picture. It brings into focus what arthritis specialists have known for some time. "An important consideration often forgotten in the planning of treatment is the enlistment of the patient's own efforts to help himself," said Dr. Ralph H. Boots of the Columbia Presbyterian Hospital.

If any victory is to be won in the battle against arthritic suffering, it can only be with the complete understanding and co-operation of the sufferer himself. In home care it is you who assumes the major responsibility for carrying out physical therapy regularly and conscientiously.

The importance of your mental attitude

Are you an exacting individual, one who is never at all satisfied with yourself or with the progress you are making with your job or with things in general?

The *perfectionist* in whatever work he does, the man or woman with the high standards no matter what the job, even if it be only housework, *is the individual who is most likely to come down with the disease.*

Herein lies a medical paradox. While it is the superior individual who is the likely candidate for an arthritis attack, it is also the superior individual who can rise above the frightening threats of the disease and marshal his mental and emotional all to counteract the effects of arthritis.

And can't you manage a smile, even though you do have arthritis? If, *just once,* you could see a light side to your problem of pain and disability you would double—triple—your chances of recovery.

Learn to smile at arthritis the way these two little girls did.

Paula S. and Diana B., both fourteen years old, found themselves in adjoining beds in the hospital after the painful hand of arthritis gripped them. They were young and very much aware of the wonder of life. They could be excused if they were less able to understand their misfortune than older people might be. You could forgive them and feel sorry for them if they lay between the white sheets tearful and not caring. You would almost expect them to be confused, shocked, and despondent.

But they weren't. Somehow, these young girls forgot their pains and forgot their disabilities long enough to chuckle at themselves. They wrote a song about arthritis.

Here are a couple of the verses:

Up in the morning
Out of our beds,
Crying because we have pain,
Cause that miserable ol' pain
Has nothing to do
But roll around our joints all day.

Oh, Lord above
Can't you hear us crying,
Tears are in our eyes;
Send down those pills
With the silver lining,
Or take us to paradise.

Not bad for fourteen-year-olds with arthritis, wouldn't you say? You may not feel like writing a song, but get rid of that downcast feeling.

Fear crippled Mrs. W., not arthritis

Had Mrs. W. taken her arthritis less seriously, she would not be the bedridden invalid that she is. Her home too would be the pleasant cheerful home it once was.

Mrs. W. had for many years been active socially in her community and had also been a well-loved leader of numerous worthwhile causes. Now, at hardly more than 50, she is bedridden and through with life. *She is crippled more by her fear of arthritis than by the disease itself.*

Her arthritis did not build up slowly over the years as it so often does. It came on suddenly. Practically overnight severe pains developed in her hands and her fingers. Her shoulders and her knees were also involved.

Unlike many arthritics, Mrs. W. sought out an arthritis specialist immediately. She had for nearly a dozen years been a volunteer in a home for incurables. She appreciated the value of prompt medical attention. She knew well the consequences of neglected diseases.

Up to this point she was behaving well under the threat of arthritic suffering. But then she lost her head—and doomed herself.

Mrs. W. was upset about her illness when she first saw her doctor. Although he explained that her arthritis was not too serious and that she could be helped, she still remained depressed. She was worried that her condition would not improve. She was afraid that she would become crippled just like the cripples she had helped at the home for incurables.

With the passing of each week, Mrs. W. became more depressed. Three months later her gloom deepened so that she completely withdrew into her own little world. She became pre-occupied only with herself and her pains. Nothing else seemed to matter. No one else seemed to exist.

It wasn't long before the once vibrant personality that had been Mrs. W. was no more. The woman who had once loved people so had removed herself from all contact with them. The once gay hostess who was quick to give a party for any worthy cause was no longer interested in social activities. The once proud and very particular housewife had lost all interest and all sense of responsibility. Her husband had to take over complete care of the home.

Mrs. W. had collapsed into a state of helplessness. She had become an *emotional cripple* because of exaggerated fears of becoming a physical cripple. The tragedy of it all was that, even at this point, her arthritis was not severe and her physical condition hardly serious.

The way you react to your illness will have a marked effect upon your recovery and the course the disease may take, as well as on your future readjustment. Unless you understand the form of arthritis you have and unless you join whole-heartedly with your doctors in their treatment of you, treatment and rehabilitation will fail.

One arthritis specialist even goes further and contends that unless you show a desire to understand, the doctor should not even accept you as a patient!

These figures prove something

That the person with arthritis is an essential teammate of the physician in medicine's successful attack against arthritis is not entirely a new concept. It was long suspected, though not fully appreciated until recently.

Research scientists, in attempting to pin down the exact

role of the arthritis sufferer in his own recovery, deliberately selected persons who had had the disease for many years. For this study group they selected persons whose limbs had been badly deformed by the disease and persons whose deformities had confined them to bed or a wheel chair.

They did this because they knew that the person who had had arthritis for many years progressively had relinquished his self-sufficiency and had gradually become more and more dependent upon others. The treatment and the rehabilitation of such a person would certainly be a challenge. The problem would be unlike any other ever faced in medicine. For to abruptly halt the effects of a hopeless disease and to suddenly change the patient's entire outlook on life would indeed be difficult, to say the least.

Patients in the study group received a complete orientation as to the form of the disease they had and the problem they faced. From the outset, every effort was made to dispel any false hopes for a cure of damaged limbs. At the same time there was a strong attempt made to arouse in them an honest appreciation for what was being done.

The results that were obtained by the two-year study were a revelation to all of medicine.

Eighty per cent of the severely crippled arthritics had been discharged from the hospital. Half of that 80% had been released as being totally self-sufficient. Their performance of daily functions at home and at work was classified as being perfectly normal. The other half were discharged as being partially self-sufficient with an average increase of 26% in the ability to perform everyday activity.

Of the less severely disabled arthritics, all had been discharged from the hospital by the time the two-year study had ended. Eighty per cent of these patients had been restored to total self-sufficiency and more than 30% had been placed in full-time jobs, many of them returning to gainful employment for the first time in several years.

There can be no doubt that modern medicine can do a great deal for you. But it is equally certain that you can do an awful lot for yourself, if you have the right mental attitude. *Courage* to hope and believe that you can lick arthritic suffering; *understanding* of arthritis and its treatment so you can work at home; *perseverance* in the Home Care Program to get its full benefits—these are the things you must hold in your mind.

Mrs. Louise G. was teaching in an area where the teacher shortage was especially acute. When arthritis hit her right elbow, right shoulder and finger joints, she tried to shrug off the pain and swelling so she could stick to her job. She could take it.

But soon she could hardly lift her arm and she had trouble even holding a piece of chalk. "I had to keep smiling for the children," she said, "but the pain was so bad that I often took fourteen aspirin a day." When she could no longer keep her records, another teacher did it for her. It was even arranged that the children should correct their own papers, using answer books. The principal of the school was understanding; he helped her as much as he could and gave her pep talks.

But at last she gave in. With her right arm useless and in a sling, she went to a doctor and asked him to sign a statement to the Board of Education to permit her to stop teaching.

"His answer was 'no!'" she said, "he told me that my children needed me, that there are too few people trained to teach children. He insisted that with faith and courage and proper treatment I could overcome my arthritis and continue to teach."

Mrs. G., with new hope, agreed, and started taking treatment. It consisted of medication to relieve the pain and swelling somewhat, followed by heat, massage, and exercise.

Six weeks later, Mrs. G. was back in front of her class again. The arthritis hadn't completely left her body, but it was under control and she was continuing a normal and very useful life. On Graduation Day she triumphantly autographed the classbooks of 115 seniors.

Afterwards, she would sometimes shudder a little when she remembered how close she had come to giving up. She knew that her recovery had started the day she decided she *could* recover.

Home care is not a substitute

What you will find in these chapters are the basic and most commonly used methods of home care that are prescribed regularly by leading arthritis specialists. Though the program is for your guidance and use, you should by all means consult your doctor and ask him to point out the specific physiotherapy treatments and exercises best suited to your particular problem.

It is important that home care be started at the proper time, usually when the pain has subsided. Started too soon, exercise in particular may harm you. Started too late, many forms of physiotherapy may do you little good. Begun at the right moment and continued until your arthritis has completely disappeared, home care can stop the pain, put you back on your feet, and restore you to a useful life.

Home care is not a poor substitute for something else. For many individuals and perhaps for you, too, home care is the most desirable form of treatment available.

REMEMBER THESE POINTS
ABOUT HOME CARE

✔ 1. All arthritis specialists agree on this: for most arthritics a program of care, *at home*, is the best way to treat arthritis.

✔ 2. You probably know how expensive a disease arthritis can be. Home care brings you the benefits of physical therapy without the continuing expense of professional help.

✔ 3. The good effects of physical therapy are built up through daily repetition. Nowhere but in your home can you achieve the day-to-day benefits of rest, heat, massage, and exercise.

✔ 4. Your *mental attitude* is *very important*. If you can take your arthritis problem less seriously, you have a better chance of overcoming it.

✔ 5. In stopping the pains and returning to a full and useful life, half the battle is YOUR DESIRE. SO ENTER YOUR HOME CARE PROGRAM WITH THE FAITH THAT YOU CAN OVERCOME YOUR ARTHRITIS.

~~~ 2

REST RELIEVES PAIN
AND RESTORES ENERGY

COMPLETE BODY REST WILL PREVENT EXCESSIVE WEAR AND tear on your involved joints, lessen the pain, and at the same time strengthen your body's natural ability to fight the disease.

Complete rest is just what is implied. If you have active painful arthritis, and it is severe, then your minimum resting period should be about twelve hours a day. All of this time, most of all in the afternoon, should be spent resting in bed. These twelve hours, incidentally, are in addition to the eight or so hours you will devote to your regular night's sleep.

The amount of rest you need depends entirely upon the severity of your arthritis. Usually, a stay of two or three weeks will prove to be of great value. In some cases, four or five months may be necessary before any benefit is realized. On the other hand, many an active arthritic is able to work eight hours a day, provided he obtains sufficient rest afterwards. Your rest periods should be prescribed by your doctor.

Resting is not just lying down

There is more to rest than just going to bed and staying there. It is *how* you rest that makes all the difference between whether you come through the disease with flexed or bent joints or with straight and firm joints ready to resume their active and normal functions.

Dr. John G. Kuhns, of Robert Breck Brigham Hospital in Boston, has made this observation about rest in the treatment of arthritis: "Usually the patient with acute arthritis is confined to bed more or less constantly until the inflammation subsides somewhat. If the patient is not supervised carefully,

 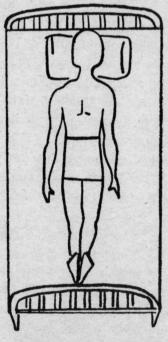

Wrong! Joints bent and contracted.   *Right! Joints comfortably straight.*

deformity may arise from the way in which the patient lies in bed."

The average individual usually likes to curl up when he rests. You, too, no doubt find that you are more comfortable in bed lying on your side with your knees bent and your legs partially drawn up.

But to bend a joint and to keep it inactive for any great length of time is to invite disaster. Not only will inactive muscles lose their strength but should you permit those that surround an arthritic joint to contract, it will lead to further pain and disability.

The proper way for you to rest is to remain flat on your back, keeping all of your joints straight. Fingers, wrists, elbows and knees must remain comfortably straight whenever you rest, throughout the night as well as the mid-day nap. At first this will be difficult and seem practically impossible. After you try it several times, however, you will not only find that you are more relaxed but upon arising, the aches and pains in your joints will have diminished.

Keeping your joints straight does not mean remaining stiff and rigid as if you were at attention. You wouldn't be able to maintain such a position for too long without becoming tired. There's a knack, a very special way to rest properly when you have rheumatoid arthritis.

Use towels for support

When you lie on your back, your body should be relaxed and at ease. While your joints should be straight, there should be no undue effort to keep them so. A folded towel under each arm and under each wrist will keep your elbows and wrists comfortably straight. Keep the palms of your hands turned upwards. A folded towel under your ankles will help keep your knees straight. At no time should you use a pillow under your knees, tempting as it may be. The use of the pillow may greatly relieve your painful knees, but it will also raise your knees and help fix them in a bent position, thus endangering your ability to walk.

Folded towels just above elbow, under wrists, and ankles help you rest.

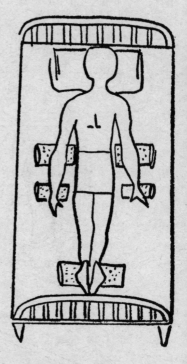

You may, if you wish, use a small pillow beneath your head, but not if you have rheumatoid arthritis of the spine. Should your spine be involved, a folded towel placed between your shoulder blades will ease your back and keep the spinal column in a natural and straight position.

A footboard and sandbags help, too

It may also be necessary that you make use of a footboard and sandbags to keep your feet straight. When lying on

your back, feet have a tendency to turn out, thus putting a
strain on your knees. Your feet will also turn out under the
weight of your bed covers. The footboard will keep the bed covers off your feet while the sandbags placed against the out-
sides of your feet will help keep them straight, thus easing the
stress upon your knees.

Both the footboard and the sandbags can easily be made at
home. The board should be about four or five inches wide and
about 24 inches long. A six- or eight-inch wing nailed to each
end will permit the board to stand on edge across the foot of

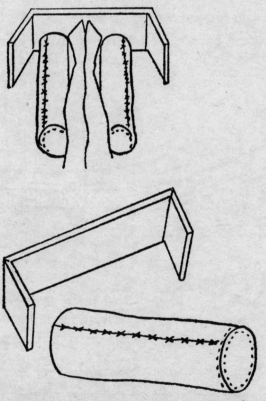

Home-made sandbags and footboard.

the bed in a box-like position that will keep the weight of the covers off your feet. The flat of the board should rest against the soles of your feet.

The sandbags can also be made at home. A sturdy cloth may be used. However, you will find light canvas to be more durable and easier to handle. Each bag should be large enough to hold your feet straight. A bag about 10 inches wide and 20 inches long that could rest against the outside of your foot and the lower leg, from the footboard to about the knee, will prove highly effective.

How to firm up a saggy mattress

Chances are too that you will need a bedboard. Generally, modern beds are far too soft, especially for arthritics. Instead

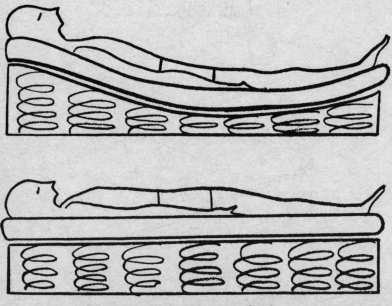

A sagging mattress is bad.

of keeping your spine straight and in good alignment, a soft mattress will give where the weight is greatest. As a result, your spine will take on the curves the mattress is creating for it. Your hips also will sink and your hip joints will bend. It is because of this that you so often awaken with a backache and a feeling of not having rested at all.

A bedboard placed between the mattress and the bed springs will give your body proper support and maintain your spine and hips in a reasonably straight position. Though bedboards can be bought in any department or furniture store,

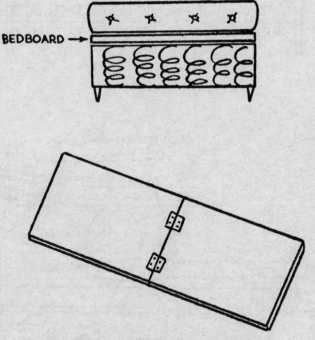

BEDBOARD →

Put a home-made bedboard between mattress and spring. Hinges make it easier to handle.

they can easily be made at home from three-quarter-inch plywood. The board should be large enough to run the full length and width of the bed. To facilitate handling, it is suggested the bedboard consist of two halves held together by hinges.

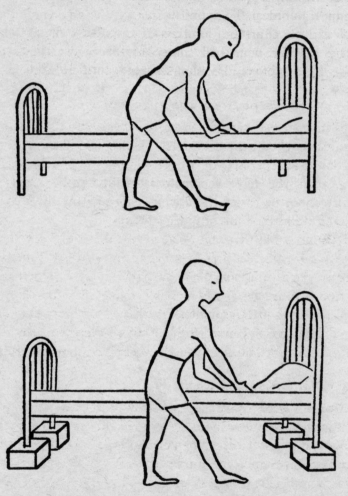

Blocks will raise your bed to a comfortable height.

Bed too low? Raise it

Modern beds are also as a rule too low. Getting in and out of them usually calls for the use of many joints and for quite a lot of bending, stooping, and lifting. For the arthritic, this can be quite an ordeal. To permit you to get in and out of your bed with as little effort and joint action as possible, it may be necessary to raise your bed somewhat. Six-by-six blocks placed under the legs of your bed should give it sufficient height.

Alternate bed rest with chair rest

Resting in bed can get to be quite wearisome. And so with the first signs that the disease has begun to subside, your doctor no doubt will permit you to get off the bed and into a chair. But when you have rheumatoid arthritis, even sitting in a chair cannot be casual. Like lying in bed, sitting in a chair for you must take the form of therapeutic rest.

It is advisable that you do not remain off the bed too long at any one time. Sitting in a chair will produce stiffness and fatigue when overdone. You will find that several shorter stays off the bed are far more advisable than fewer and longer absences. Ten to fifteen minutes in a chair, four or five times a day, are all that you will need to help relieve the monotony of continued bed rest and give you the feeling of motion again.

Not just any old chair

Most modern chairs are too low for the arthritis sufferer as they make it necessary to flex the hips far more than pain will allow. To make it easier for you to sit and rise again without too much assistance and hip bending, it will be necessary to increase the height of the chair you will use. Three- to four-inch blocks under the legs should raise it to a comfortable level.

Blocks allow you to adjust chair height.

The chair should also have a flat seat and a broad, straight and uncurved high back. Its arms should be adjusted to a comfortable height in keeping with the length of your back.

Other ways of resting

Though you may require rest, it may not be necessary that you be confined to a bed. A daily two-hour rest period upon a couch, preferably during the early afternoon, may provide you with sufficient rest and still permit you to go about your everyday activities. To make certain though that you do get enough rest to offset the energy you expend during the day, you should also go to bed early, immediately after dinner, to make possible 10 to 12 hours of sleep and rest each night.

As you go about your business during the day, you should also make every effort to relieve your arthritic joints of any unnecessary strain and to provide them every opportunity to rest. For example, avoid climbing stairs, if your knees, feet, or hips are affected. If any of your other weight-bearing joints are inflamed, try to remain off the involved limbs until the acute and painful stage of the disease has passed.

Should only your hands, fingers, or wrists be involved, it

may be possible to sufficiently rest these particular joints by wearing a splint at intervals during the day and throughout the night. Light plaster and aluminum splints can be fashioned by your doctor to suit your particular needs and to keep your affected fingers, hands, or wrists properly straight.

A common misconception is that splints may increase the chances of deformity. Instinctively you want to keep your joints as active as possible in the hope that this will prevent stiffening and eventual crippling. The truth is just the reverse. It is over-activity and overuse that will keep your joints in a perpetual state of inflammation, thus adding to their disability and increasing the possibility of crippling. Rest in a splint, on the other hand, will decrease joint inflammation and lessen pain and the risk of deformity.

At first, perhaps, your splinted joint may begin to feel a bit stiff. This is due to the inactivity of the muscles and the tendons of the joint. Heat, massage, and exercise will help you overcome this temporary discomfort and at the same time help retain the joint's range of motion. If a splint is prescribed for you, wear it as directed by your doctor. Do not keep your joint in a splint all the time, as this will only weaken the joint's muscular structure and add to your problem.

Your doctor may decide to permit you to discard your splints during convalescence, when pain and swelling will have subsided and recovery will be but a matter of weeks away. However, because your joints may still need added support and protection, a firm elastic cotton bandage will in most instances provide adequate splinting. Should additional security be needed, felt sheets or sheet cotton rollers may be applied beneath the bandage. This type of joint support is only temporary and should not be used for acutely and severely inflamed joints.

Balance rest by exercise

Important as rest may be, rest alone cannot accomplish the one desired result of physical medicine and home care, that of maintaining the power of movement in your affected joints. For that matter, it is quite easy to overdo rest, thus adding to your problem. For example, the muscles of a joint that has been at complete rest in a splint for a prolonged period will become so weakened that when the splint is finally removed the joint will have no support at all.

To be at all effective, rest must be balanced by exercise. (A detailed program of home care exercises is contained in a later chapter.) As the condition of your joints improves, the amount of rest you will need will decrease while your need for therapeutic exercise will increase. A proper balance is the minimum amount of rest needed to enable you to resume the maximum amount of activity you are able to perform without experiencing muscle stiffness and pain. In other words, the least amount of rest necessary to make possible the greatest amount of activity with ease and comfort.

REMEMBER THESE POINTS
ABOUT REST

✔ 1. Correct body rest lessens pain, strengthens your natural disease resistance, and prevents excessive wear and tear.

✔ 2. DON'T MAKE THIS MISTAKE:
   Too many arthritics think that rest is just lying down or taking it easy. THAT'S WRONG!

✔ 3. Body rest for the arthritis sufferer is a scientific procedure. You must learn this procedure. The detailed instructions in this chapter will teach you.

(pages 40-42 combined on this page)

3

GOOD POSTURE WILL LESSEN ARTHRITIC MISERIES

It is essential that you maintain good posture at all times. Good posture will help prevent fatigue, the one factor that every arthritic can well do without.

Dr. Boots has said that "Fatigue is one of the greatest contributing or precipitating factors of all disease. The elimination of fatigue will do much to restore the mental and physical endurance of individuals with rheumatoid arthritis."

Good posture will also lessen the strain upon inflamed joints and distressed muscles, ease pain, and reduce the chances of deformity and crippling.

As an arthritic you probably suffer from poor posture. As soon as you instinctively try to protect your involved joints you assume poor posture. Sitting too long in one spot just to avoid using your painful knees, for example, will cause far greater pain and stiffness and even increase the chances of crippling. That is why, when you must go on a long automobile ride, you should stop once in a while to get out and stretch and walk around a bit.

What bad posture does to your body

The extensive damage that may take place just because you are not standing or sitting properly is at times fantastic. It all starts with the simple fact that when posture is bad the various parts of your body are not being held in proper alignment by your muscles.

The muscles that tire first are those that hold your body erect against the pull of gravity. As muscular fatigue sets in, the

Bad posture can do fantastic damage.

ligaments that support the joints of the spine and the limbs become overstretched. The result is sprain, a condition in which the surfaces of the joints are no longer parallel. With the alignment of the joint now impaired, any added pressure results in friction and irritation within the joint. Changes in the ligaments and bones may follow and deformities may develop.

Poor posture will also disturb many of the internal organs, especially those within the abdominal cavity. The function of the diaphragm may be interfered with. All of this makes for greater stress not only upon the entire system but upon already irritated arthritic joints. Further irritation and the possibility of serious deformity are thus increased.

Take a look at yourself

Now, you may argue that there is nothing wrong with your posture, and you may be right. But test yourself; stand naked before your dresser mirror.

Stand sideways, at right angles to the mirror. Stand as you do normally, relaxed and at ease. It does not matter whether your body faces to the right or the left. Now, turn your head and look past your shoulder at your reflection. Is your head somewhat forward? Are your shoulders rounded? Is your chest sunken? Is your abdomen prominent? Does the small of your back curve in considerably? Well, if the answer to any one of these questions is "yes," it probably is also "yes" to two or three of the remaining four. Whether it is one yes or more, you will have to accept the fact that your posture is poor, perhaps poor enough to affect your arthritis quite severely.

And remember what Dr. Kuhns has observed about the posture of arthritics: "Faulty posture is found in almost every patient suffering from chronic arthritis. Its correction aids in preventing recurrence of disability in arthritis."

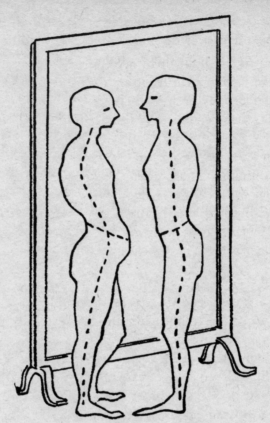

*A mirror will help you test
your posture.*

When posture is good, there is no exaggerated curve to the spine. You stand as tall or lie as straight as you possibly can. The chest, while naturally relaxed during normal breathing, is not flat or depressed at the waist line. The lower abdomen is flat but the upper abdomen and the chest are full and rounded, thus permitting the diaphragm to work effectively and efficiently. All this is without effort or strain.

Simple exercises do a world of good

You may find it difficult to overcome the habits of poor posture. Besides, your arthritis itself may interfere with your assuming a good body position. Despite these handicaps, you still must avoid poor posture if you are to avoid fatigue, pain, and crippling.

You can do this with postural exercises. If you will spend but 20 or 30 minutes a day doing the postural exercises in this chapter you will be able to undo much of what time and bad habits have brought about. The responsibility for carrying these exercises out rests solely with you. Doing them diligently will result in proper balance of muscle strength and eventual good posture.

Good posture develops rather slowly and often without your even being aware of it. You may not be able to see any improvement for perhaps six or more months. However, the day you look back, free of fatigue and pain and general misery, you will marvel that so much good could have come about in so simple a way and in so short a time.

Arthritic exercises are specialized

There are any number of postural exercises you may find quite helpful. Those that are described here are not only basic but they have been devised to strengthen the very muscles and joints undermined by your arthritis attack. The effort to improve your posture is a continual thing, a part of your very treatment. It goes without saying, therefore, that you must take these exercises seriously, for much of your improvement will depend upon how well you do them and how faithfully you follow them through.

When you start your exercises, keep in mind any limitations

the disease has placed upon you. Do not try to force your way through an exercise just for the sake of exercising. If you find that any particular motion causes you undue pain, stop right then and there. If any deformity you have does not permit you to complete a maneuver as perfectly as it is written, let it go at that. It is entirely permissible and even advisable at times for you to modify any of the following exercises to conform to your ability to perform them. As you improve and your range of motion increases, your ability to complete each exercise properly will come quite naturally and easily.

Although postural exercises usually are associated with an upright position and with persons who can get about, a number of the exercises described here are to be done lying down. This will enable you to make profitable use of these exercises even though you may still be confined to your bed. Four of the exercises, however, have been especially designed for the bedridden arthritic.

Start and end each exercise period with the following deep-breathing session: Keep your chin in, breathe deeply and raise your chest. Hold chest up and exhale by drawing your abdomen in and up. Relax and repeat for several minutes.

The first three of the following exercises are the most important. Upon these are based many of the others. You may start your exercises by doing each of these two times at a session, two sessions each day. As your range of motion increases, gradually increase the number of times you do each exercise until you are able to do each with ease from three to ten times, twice a day. As your strength improves, slowly add the other exercises until you are able to perform most or all of them from three to ten times each, twice a day. Do not try to do any of these exercises more than that.

TEN BASIC POSTURE EXERCISES

• *Exercise 1.* Lie face up on your bed. Straighten out the curve in your lower back by getting your back as flat against the bed as possible. Tighten your buttock muscles. Pull in your abdominal muscles, flattening your abdomen at the same time. Do not hold your breath. Release your buttock muscles, then your abdominal muscles, and repeat.

• *Exercise 2.* Lie face down. Place a pillow under your abdomen and repeat the above exercise.

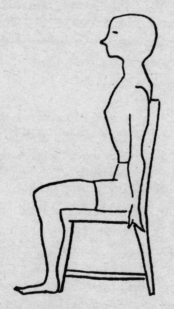

Exercise 1 can be done in a chair if you prefer.

• *Exercise 3.* Lie on your back. Clasp your hands in back of your neck and repeat Exercise No. 1. Then, as you release your buttock and abdominal muscles, slowly bend one knee, sliding the foot back. Hold this position for a moment and then slowly slide the foot forward until both legs are equally extended.

• *Exercise 4*. Lie on your back. Place your hands behind your head and flex your knees. Keep your back flat and your chin in. Breathe deeply, elevating your chest. Maintain this elevated position of the chest for a moment. Exhale, holding your lower abdomen in.

Slowly slide foot back, then forward. (Exercise 3.)

• *Exercise 5*. Lie on your back. Cross your arms on your chest. Tighten your buttock muscles and pull in your abdomen. Raise your head and shoulders from the bed for a count of six.

• *Exercise 6*. Lie on your back. Keep your hands at your sides. Tighten your buttock muscles and pull in your abdomen. Raise your arms over your head and inhale. Lower your arms and exhale. Remember to keep your back flat.

• *Exercise 7*. Lie on your back. Keep your arms at your sides. Tighten your buttock muscles and pull in your abdomen. Roll your arms outward turning your palms upward and forcing your shoulders back at the same time. Keep your lower back and the back of your neck against the bed. Keep your chin in.

• *Exercise 8.* Lie on your back. Place your hands in back of your neck. Tighten your buttock muscles and pull in your abdomen. Keep your legs perfectly straight. Raise and lower your left leg. Repeat with your right leg. Then, slowly alternate, raising and lowering one leg at a time.

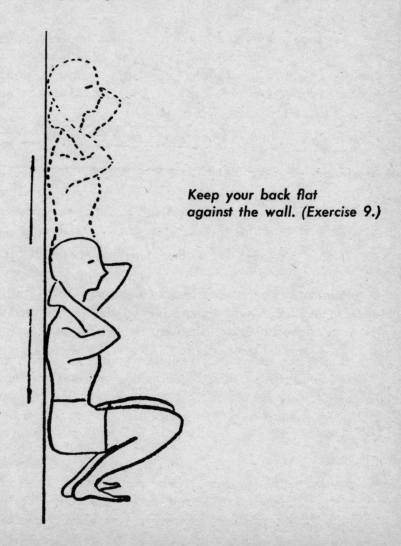

Keep your back flat against the wall. (Exercise 9.)

• *Exercise 9.* Stand with your back against the wall. Keep your heels three inches from the wall and your feet three inches apart. Place your hands in back of your neck. Bend your knees, tighten your buttock muscles and pull in your abdomen, keeping your back flat against the wall. Straighten your knees, and repeat.

• *Exercise 10.* Lie face down. Place a pillow under your abdomen. Place your arms shoulder high and bend your elbows, forming a right angle. Tighten your buttock muscles, pull in your abdomen, raise your arms and hands from the bed, bringing your shoulder blades together.

FOUR PASSIVE EXERCISES FOR THE BEDRIDDEN

If you are confined to your bed and find that the above ten exercises are somewhat difficult for you, the following positions and passive exercises will help you improve your posture.

• *Exercise 1.* Lie on your back. There should be no pillow under your head. Place a pillow under your upper back and under your knees. Put your hands under the back of your head and maintain this position for 20 or 30 minutes after each meal.

• *Exercise 2.* Lie face down. Place a pillow under your abdomen. Keep your legs straight. Place your arms on the bed above your head. Keep this position for 20 to 30 minutes three times a day immediately after you have finished position No. 1, above.

• *Exercise 3.* Lie on your back. Slowly stretch your body to the left. Keep the lower back flat against the bed permitting only your upper back and shoulders to move slightly with the stretch. This action should separate your ribs from your pelvis.

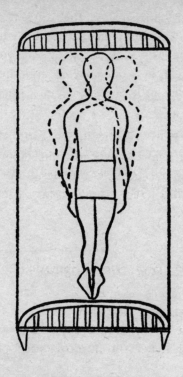

Move only the upper part of your body. (Exercise 3.)

Return to normal position and repeat with a slow easy stretch to the right. Alternate several times.

• *Exercise 4.* Lie on your back. Place your hands on the frontal section of your lower ribs. Breathe deeply and with your fingers pull the lower ribs up and out. Don't relax your hands. Slowly exhale and maintain the pull on your lower ribs. Repeat several times without releasing the upward and outward pull.

Be conscious of your posture

Once you are on your feet, you should make every effort to maintain your posture as best you can. A good posture when standing is to keep your feet pointing forward with your weight carried on the outer side of the feet. Keep your lower abdomen in and your lower back flat, just as you did when carrying out your exercises in bed. Keep your head erect and your chin in.

When getting around for the first time after a long rest in bed, temporary support may be necessary to help you maintain good body alignment. A properly fitted corset or spinal braces are often used. These, however, are worn only when you are up and about. They are removed at night and during exercise. They are discarded as soon as your body is able to maintain good posture without any assistance.

REMEMBER THESE POINTS
ABOUT GOOD POSTURE

✔ 1. *If your body isn't "stacked" correctly, you are aggravating your arthritis.*
✔ 2. Be aware of your posture whether sitting, standing, or lying down.
✔ 3. You may not think that you have bad posture, but doctors have found that MOST arthritics HAVE.
✔ 4. Check your posture by standing sideways in front of a mirror.
✔ 5. Then correct your posture by diligent application of the exercises contained in this chapter.

(pages 54-56 combined on this page)

~~~ 4

HEAT SOOTHES PAIN
AND FREES
TIGHT JOINTS

HEAT IS A VALUABLE PART OF YOUR HOME CARE PROGRAM. It will rest your arthritic joints by lessening their aches and pains, and it will prepare you for the essential therapeutic exercises that are to follow. It is heat, too, that will make it possible for you to move your involved joints through a greater range of motion, thus not only preventing crippling but also correcting any deformities that may have begun.

Dr. Bowie definitely states that "Heat is one of the most useful weapons available in the treatment of arthritis. When possible, apply heat to the affected joints several times per day."

Heat should not be applied during the acute stage of the disease when the stricken joints are highly inflamed. Heat at this time will often aggravate the joints and increase the pain and

57

discomfort. Should pain develop during or after heat therapy, you should discontinue the treatment immediately. Your joints may not be ready for heat.

Generally, heat should be applied for no more than 20 or 30 minutes at a time and not more than twice a day. Your doctor, for particular reasons, may decide to prescribe a longer and a more frequent exposure to heat therapy, but don't try to do it yourself. Often when pain follows the application of heat, it is because too much heat has been applied. Often, it may be desirable to follow heat treatment with gentle massage and exercise, instructions for which are given later.

Use the right method for your problem

There are numerous ways of applying heat. The method you will use will depend a great deal upon the location of your arthritis and upon how widespread it is. For example, a heat lamp will give you a good concentration of heat over a small area and so is ideal for treating a single joint. A lamp, however, is practically useless if you must apply heat to several joints at a time, let's say to the fingers, wrist, and elbow of the same arm or to the knee and ankle of the same leg. In such an instance, you would have to use a baker. Yet, a baker becomes a rather clumsy device to use when your shoulder is involved. It is important, therefore, that the method you use be carefully selected to conform with your particular problem.

Heat must be used correctly

Although heat is a simple form of therapy, its *haphazard* application can be harmful. Besides, there are certain persons who cannot tolerate heat. Extreme caution must be used in giving heat treatments to a diabetic, for example. Persons with weak blood circulation or with scars must be treated with great care. Those who have subnormal sensations and so cannot realize they are being subjected to too much heat also must be closely watched. *Check with your doctor to be sure.*

INFRARED HEAT LAMP

Perhaps the easiest way to apply dry luminous heat to an arthritic joint is with an infrared lamp. These lamps have been standardized and are available at most drug and department stores. A single-unit floor model is the most desirable.

Using the infrared lamp

Do not sit too close to the lamp. At no time should the lamp be closer than 18 inches from the joint under treatment. If you find at the first trial that you are unable to tolerate the dry heat, check with your doctor. He may advise you to apply a wet compress to the joint while it is under the lamp. When the moisture in the compress evaporates, wet the toweling again.

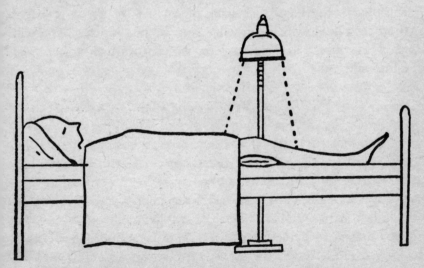

The lamp should never be closer than eighteen inches.

At first, do not attempt to remain under the lamp for too long a period. A few minutes at a time at the start may be all that you will be able to tolerate. After several sessions under the lamp, you may set a time limit of about 10 to 15 minutes. At no time should you be under the lamp for more than 30 minutes. Let your own comfort be your guide and make certain your skin does not burn.

How to make an infrared unit

You can make a simple and highly effective infrared unit yourself. The infrared bulb, a therapeutic Mazda 250-watt lamp, can be bought at almost any drugstore. At a photography store buy a clamp-on reflector that is used for photoflood lighting. The reflector consists of a round aluminum shield, a socket, and a clamp that can be attached to the top of a chair, to the edge of a door, to a molding or almost anywhere. Because of the weight of the bulb, you should find a fairly secure and sufficiently broad base upon which to fasten the clamp so the unit will not come crashing to the floor. The back of a chair set about two feet from the one in which you will sit or the bed in which you will lie is the most desirable base on which to attach a clamp-on lamp unit.

HOME BAKING

For a long time baking was considered a hospital or a clinical procedure. In the past few years, however, arthritis specialists have come to feel that their patients can handle baking in their homes quite efficiently and with little difficulty. Bakers can be purchased in a number of sizes. A simple baking apparatus that can be made at home has also proved quite useful and effective.

Using the baker unit

When you first start using the baker, never remain under it for more than 10 to 15 minutes at a time. After several days you will be able to gradually increase the time until a baking session will last a maximum of 30 minutes. You should never force yourself, however, to observe the half-hour maximum when you find that your joints are unable to stand the heat. Your own tolerance should be your guide; you should never insist on exposing yourself to heat that cannot be borne with comfort. Watch your joints carefully when they are under the baker. Never permit the skin to burn or to blister. Make sure that at no time is your skin in contact with the lighted bulbs. With either of the two home-made baking units to be described here, you are able to control the amount of heat merely by lighting the desired number of bulbs.

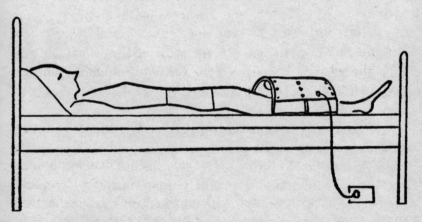

At first, use the baker for ten-minute periods.

When you come out from under the baker, be careful not to expose yourself to any chill. Do not permit the heated sections to cool off too quickly. Follow each baking session with mas-

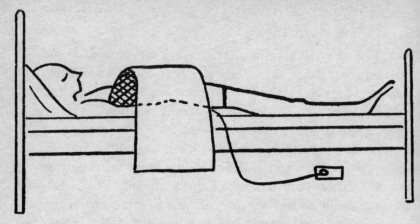

Baker No. 2 is simply covered with a blanket.

sage. After massage, rest in bed for an amount of time that is equal to the time spent under the baker plus the time spent on massage.

How to build a baking unit

Baker No. 1—Materials: a frame made of ³⁄₁₆ by ⅝ inch strap iron, a highly polished strip of tin sheeting, two double back-to-back light-bulb sockets, four 60-watt electric bulbs, and about 6 or 8 feet of rubber-insulated wire.

Arch the strap-iron frame so that it forms a tunnel-like structure 18 inches in height and 24 inches in width. The depth of the structure should be about 24 to 30 inches. Place the metal sheeting over the top of the frame, permitting about 6 inches of it to come down each side of the arch. Rivet the sheeting into place or fasten it with stove bolts. Attach the double sockets beneath the center of the arched tin roof. Wire the sockets in multiple so that two lamps can be turned on independently of the other two.

If you are not handy with sheet-metal work or if you are un-

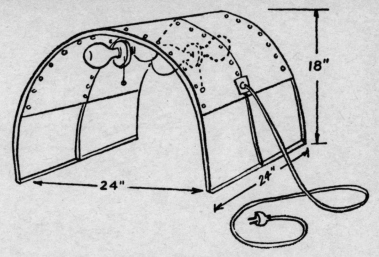

A baking unit, inexpensive and easy to make.

able to find a metal-work shop to help you fashion the baker, you can make several variations of this particular model by arching the tin reflector over a simple square tunnel-like wooden frame or by making the entire tunnel out of solid wood and fitting a piece of tin on the underside of the arch as a reflector.

This baker as well as the one described below is high enough to permit you to insert your arms or your legs with ease and comfort.

Baker No. 2—Materials: a sheet of wire fencing about 6 feet in length by 2 or 2½ feet in width, two double back-to-back light-bulb sockets, four 60-watt electric bulbs, and about 6 or 8 feet of rubber-insulated lamp wire.

Bend the fencing into an arch or a tunnel-like structure. The curved roof of the tunnel should be about 16 to 18 inches high and the width about 24 inches. The length or depth of the tunnel will be the width of the fencing. Fasten the two double sockets to the underside of the tunnel roof.

To keep the heat concentrated, one or two heavy blankets are

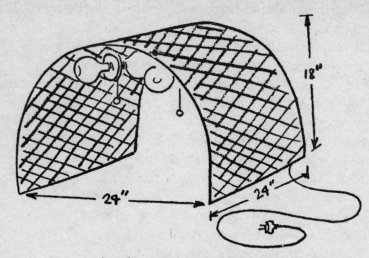

Another type of baking unit.

placed over the entire baker. The heat can be controlled, as in the other baker, by the number of bulbs you choose to light.

The insulation provided by the blankets permits you to pre-heat this type of baker. Cover the baker completely with the blankets, including the open tunnel ends. Light all four bulbs for several minutes until the temperature within is at the desired level. Before you insert your arm or your leg, extinguish three of the four bulbs. You will find that the desired heat level will be maintained for quite a while.

HOT WATER BOTTLE

Perhaps the most common device for the application of heat is the hot water bottle. Older variations are the oven-warmed brick wrapped in a blanket and the oven-heated cloth bag filled with sand. One advantage of the bottle is that you are able to control the amount of heat emanating from it. Make sure that the water you fill the bottle with is never any hotter than 116 degrees F.

If you use the hot brick or the hot bag of sand, you should be especially careful that neither of these come in direct contact with your skin. You should take special caution when these hot objects are placed over scar tissue or over an area where the sensory nerves are weakened, thus preventing you from being warned in time should your skin burn.

Even when using an ordinary hot water bag, you still must be careful. There is always the danger of burning yourself if you permit the bag or the metal parts to come in direct contact with your skin. A good precaution is to wrap the bag or the bottle in a towel of desired thickness. As the contents of the bag cool, the toweling can be removed a layer at a time.

ELECTRIC PAD

In many homes, the electric pad has replaced the hot water bottle as a means of providing therapeutic heat. Modern pads do have many advantages over the hot water bottle. Perhaps, the principal one is that the heat from an electric pad can be kept at a constant pre-selected level. Then too, the pad is more convenient to use. It can, for example, be wrapped around a joint without any trouble.

Though an electric pad is equipped with a thermostat or some other heat-control device, you still should not relax your caution. The chances of burning yourself are slight, but it may be wise to keep in mind the degrees of heat that the low, medium, and high markings on the pad's control dial stand for. These temperatures are seldom given on the dial and are much higher than you realize. Low is 108 degrees F.; medium, 180 degrees F.; and high is 245 degrees F. In the treatment of arthritis, it is best that the dial be always maintained at low heat. Even then, it may be necessary that you wrap the involved joint in a towel to prevent burns.

HOT AIR

A hand-type home hair dryer is a simple and effective device for applying dry heat. The small blower makes possible an excellent hot-air douche when attached to a stand or to the back of a chair. Hot air may be blown with good results against any painful joint, but is especially helpful in treating the fingers and the hands. Hot-air treatments may last from 10 to 30 minutes at a time and may be repeated several times a day.

When using a hot-air blower, do not hold it by hand. It should be kept on the stand that comes with it so that its distance from the affected joint will always remain constant. This will prevent overheating the arthritic trouble-spot. You will find that sitting up in a chair will prove to be the best position for a hot-air douche.

The area covered by the hot-air dryer is limited. This may make it necessary for you to continually change your position in front of the blower so as to permit the hot air to reach all sides of the involved joint. Should this be necessary, don't forget to add up your treatment time so that you will not remain under the blower for more than 30 minutes at a time. Always be careful not to chill the section of the joint that is not facing the blower.

PARAFFIN BATHS

Hot paraffin provides an effective means for applying concentrated heat to individual joints, especially those of the hands and feet. It permits a uniform application of heat around an entire joint, at the same time holding the heat constant for quite a while afterwards. This medium is especially useful for relieving the severe pain that accompanies chronic rheumatoid arthritis and the painful swelling that so often strikes the hand and fingers. Once the paraffin is removed, the joint will be left moist and soft and in ideal condition for massage, stretching, and gentle corrective exercise.

Paraffin is an economical medium. The material can be remelted innumerable times thus permitting its repeated use. It's never thrown away after treatment. Paraffin baths at home should be used several times a day.

How to prepare and use paraffin

Hot paraffin should be used with care. As with any other heat-retaining substance, the risk of burning yourself is always present. In this instance you are placing a hot waxy material in direct contact with inflamed and sore joints that may be highly

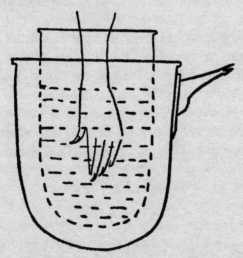

Your hand must not move during paraffin application.

sensitive to heat. One precaution you should take is to shave the hairy parts of your skin where treatment is to be given, so as to lessen the chance of irritation when the paraffin is removed. You should also apply cold cream or some other soothing lubricant to the area the first few times you use a paraffin bath.

Here are the materials you will need:

A double boiler from 8 to 12 inches deep or an enamel pail about 10 inches in diameter.

An electric hot plate. (Paraffin is inflammable and if you are using a gas or a coal stove you will need an asbestos pad to reduce fire hazard.)

Four pounds of canning grade paraffin.

One pound of vaseline or an equivalent amount of light mineral oil.

A bath thermometer, wax paper, and flannel cloth.

Mix the paraffin and the vaseline or oil. Heat slowly with occasional stirring. The mixture will melt at 120 to 140 degrees F. When the mixture has melted, remove from the stove and allow to cool somewhat. When a thin white coating or scum has formed on the top, the paraffin is ready to use. Place the boiler or pail on a chair or a table at a convenient height.

To apply paraffin to your fingers, hand, or wrist, maintain your hand in a relaxed natural position. Dip your hand into the melted paraffin and allow it to remain there for several seconds. Withdraw your hand and allow the layer of paraffin to harden. Repeat this procedure until about five or six coatings have been applied. The paraffin cast or glove that has been formed should be from one-fourth to one-half an inch thick. Several additional dippings may be necessary to achieve this desired thickness.

Do not move your fingers at any time while applying the

paraffin or after it has hardened. You must keep your hand still if you are to keep the paraffin coating from cracking. Wrap your paraffin hand in wax paper and then cover it with the flannel cloth so as to maintain the heat as long as possible. Keep the paraffin glove in place for about 30 minutes. Your doctor may advise you to keep the wax coating on for an hour or two. When the time is up, peel off the paraffin and place it back into the double boiler or pail for re-use. Repeat this treatment several times a day.

Paraffin can be applied with an ordinary paint brush.

The principle for applying paraffin to the shoulders, elbows, knees, or spine is the same. However, there is a slight variation in the technique. In these instances, the paraffin is applied with a soft long-haired paint brush. The brush should be about two inches wide and should not have been used for any other purpose. A large wide roll of gauze may also be used to dab on the paraffin.

HOT TUB BATHS

One of the most useful means for applying general heat at home is the hot tub bath. You will find the bath practical for heating any number of afflicted joints at the same time. What is more, the hot tub bath is highly efficient in elevating your body temperature, thus easing the overall aches and misery and the tension that so often accompany the disease. You should, if you are able, take a hot tub bath every day before you exercise.

A hot tub bath when used in the treatment of arthritis is not quite the same as the bath you normally take for cleanliness. The principal purpose of the therapeutic bath is to raise your body temperature somewhat above normal and to maintain this increase for a period of time. It is because of this, that you should be careful when taking a hot tub bath. *For unless you know what you are doing, a prolonged rise in body temperature may prove harmful.*

It is advisable that a member of your family be present while you are in the tub. You should be alert for any undue weakness or any increase in joint pain. A cool towel around your head will help lessen discomfort. Always keep a water thermometer available when you enter the tub. The temperature of the water should be 97 degrees F. While you are in the tub, gradually in-

The essentials for taking a hot tub bath.

crease this to 102 degrees F. It should never exceed 102 degrees F. without your doctor's permission and under no condition should it go beyond 105 degrees F.

Your joints, since they are inflamed, may be unduly sensitive to hot water. This is why it is suggested that you enter the tub when the water temperature is 97 degrees F., just below your own normal body temperature. The first time you take a therapeutic bath, do not remain in the tub for more than five minutes. This will give you an idea of how much heat you are able to stand. Only when you are well able to tolerate the hot water may you slowly increase your stay in the tub to 20 minutes and to 30 and 40 minutes with the permission of your doctor.

You may, if you wish, add magnesium sulphate, sodium chloride, or small amounts of pine extract to the bath water. Sodium chloride may be added at the rate of one pound for every 10 gallons of water. Incidentally, while you are in the tub, you should drink water quite freely to replace that which you lose through perspiration.

After you leave the tub, have your home care assistant spray or sponge you with tepid or cool water. This should be followed by an alcohol rubdown. After you are thoroughly dry, return to bed. Cover yourself lightly and sleep for a little while. If your doctor feels you should prolong the effect of the heat, wrap yourself in several blankets for 20 minutes immediately after you leave the hot tub. Since you will sweat profusely under the blankets, drink a great deal of fluids.

FOAM AND BUBBLE BATHS

A bubble bath will give you the same effect that you will get by bathing in the waters of many a world-famous spa, at far less cost. The value of the spa and the bubble bath is in the carbon dioxide that is contained in the water. The bubbles of carbon dioxide not only help retain natural body heat as does the foam bath, but the absorption of the carbon dioxide through the skin also provides a stimulating effect.

There are devices available that will turn your bath into a therapeutic foam or bubble bath. A foam bath is prepared by placing 10 cc. or about one-third of an ounce of saponin solution in four inches of water. Oxygen or air is forced into this shallow mixture with a special perforated tube or hose. In about 15 minutes the foam will rise sufficiently to permit you to enter the tub. The foam, which should cover your entire body, will retain your body heat close to the skin, thus inducing sweating. Foam baths are highly desirable when a sedative effect is necessary.

If you are unable to obtain the use of the above mixing apparatus, you may still enjoy a bubble bath by preparing one with the help of chemicals. Fill your tub with water no hotter than 95 degrees F. Add four pounds of table salt and one-half pound of sodium carbonate. Stir both into the water thoroughly. Then, carefully place tablets of acid sodium phosphate along the sides of the tub.

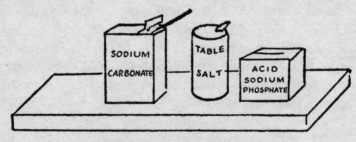

Materials for a foam bath.

You must remain perfectly still while in the tub so as to permit the carbon dioxide bubbles to cling to your body. It is also essential that you cover the entire tub with a blanket so as not to inhale the escaping gas. Your first bubble bath should not last

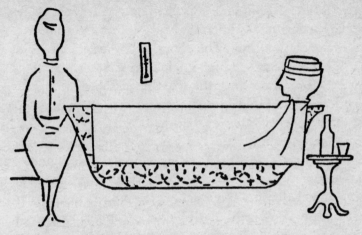

Put a blanket over the tub when taking a foam bath.

more than five minutes. Later you may slowly increase your sittings but never beyond 15 minutes. Because your own body heat is a part of the treatment, the water temperature should not be more than 95 degrees F. For that matter, as you begin to improve, the water temperature should be lowered to 86 degrees F.

WHIRLPOOL BATHS

The whirlpool bath, long a standby of hospital physiotherapy departments, is now available for home care use. This form of therapeutic bath not only makes possible a uniform application of heat but also the mild and desirable effects of gentle massage. Before you go to the trouble and expense of converting your bathtub into a whirlpool bath, it is advisable that you first find out whether the mechanical massage of the swirling water will hurt you. Your arthritic joints may be too sensitive for the agitated action of the water.

You will find the whirlpool bath highly effective in stimulating your circulation and especially useful should you have chronic rheumatoid arthritis. When you first enter the bath, the water temperature should be about 96 degrees F. Keep increasing the temperature gradually as long as you are able to tolerate the heat. Remember that the whirling action of the water also helps retain and build up heat. At no time should you permit the water to become hotter than 105 degrees F.

In a matter of minutes after you enter the bath, you will notice that your skin is becoming unusually red and warm. You will then become aware of a glowing feeling and a general easing of body tension. Your aching joints and muscles that have been tied in knots will slowly become completely relaxed and supple. You will find that you will be able to extend your contracted joints further and increase their range of motion far easier than when you were out of the water. Gentle massage and exercise is even possible while you are in the tub. A whirlpool bath treatment should last about 30 minutes and two treatments daily should be sufficient.

A simplified agitator that will turn your bathtub into an efficient whirlpool bath is now available on the market at a fairly reasonable cost. It has no moveable parts, uses no electricity and operates solely on water pressure. The small compact gadget attaches to the side of your bathtub and connects to your water faucet. But if you are resourceful or have a mechanically inclined relative in your family, you can make your own whirlpool jet unit.

A whirlpool is simple to make

A whirlpool jet can be made from standard one-inch galvanized pipe. The jet consists of two inlets connected through a T-joint with a common rubber hose leading to your faucet's mixing valve. Each of the inlets is equipped with a half-inch McCaniel suction tee, with an air-vent pipe from the tee to the

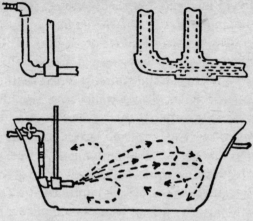

A home-made whirlpool bath.

top of the bath to provide adequate air mixing. The inlets are placed 4 and 18 inches above the bottom and near the outlet. A 2½-inch overflow outlet is placed at one end near the top to keep the water at a safe level.

CONTRAST BATHS

Contrast baths, in which arthritic joints are immersed alternately in hot and cold water, often are of value in certain states of the disease, especially when the rheumatoid process is smoldering. You will find contrast baths particularly beneficial should the doctor find you are suffering considerably from painful spasms of the blood vessels in and around your stricken joints.

Contrast baths are most useful for the treatment of the hands and feet. Though only one hand or one foot may be involved, the treatment should include the upper or lower extremities as a unit; both hands and both feet going through the alternating baths together. It is best to put the hands and the feet through the contrast procedure simultaneously. It seems that the desired increase in blood flow through the arthritic joints is far greater when the upper and lower extremities are immersed in the baths at the very same time.

Use two large buckets for the feet and two separate buckets for the hands. At the beginning, however, and until you become accustomed to the contrast-bath routine, it may be advisable that you treat your hands and feet separately. The two buckets you select should be large enough to take two upper or lower limbs together, the feet to include the legs up to the knees and the hands to include the arms up to the elbows.

Fill one bucket with hot water, no hotter than 110 degrees F., and the other bucket with cold water of about 60 or 65 degrees

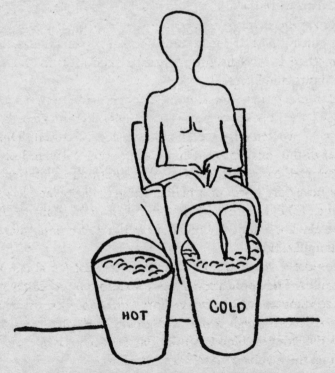

Contrast baths help to soothe pain.

F. The contrast treatment is begun by immersing the legs or the arms in the hot bath for 10 minutes. After this initial immersion, remove your arms or legs and plunge them quickly into the cold bath, holding them in the cold water for one minute. Remove and return to the hot bath for four minutes. Then, for one-half hour, alternate, four minutes in the hot bath and one minute in the cold. Complete the treatment with the hot bath.

HOT FOMENTATIONS OR COMPRESSES

Hot fomentations, commonly known as hot compresses, are quite effective in the treatment of acutely painful and swollen joints. You will also find this particular technique for applying heat especially helpful in relieving the painful, stiff joints that are so much a part of the chronic stage of rheumatoid arthritis. The method is most useful in treating such areas as the shoulders, elbows, and knees.

Hot fomentations are simple to apply. The only materials you need are a bucket of hot water of about 116 degrees F. and a piece of woolen blanket or a heavy turkish towel. Dip the blanket or the towel into the hot water, wring it dry and place it over the area to be treated. Cover the entire area immediately with a heavy dry towel or a blanket so as to keep the heat from escaping. (Should you find that the pain or swelling increases, remove the hot compress immediately and discontinue this form of heat application.)

A compress, you will find, will retain its heat for about 15 or 20 minutes. The application should therefore be repeated about every 20 minutes for one hour. Three such one-hour treatments evenly spaced through a day will provide sufficient heat to increase the flow of blood within the particular joint and also loosen up the involved muscles and tendons.

If you place a layer of wax paper over the hot compress before you cover it with a dry blanket, you will find that the heat will be retained for as long as a half hour with but a single application, thus eliminating more frequent changes of the compress. You may also add a cupful of magnesium sulphate to the hot water to provide a mild analgesic and restful effect. This substance, though, has a tendency to dry out the skin and so the use of a skin lotion after each treatment is advisable.

FULL WET PACK

The full wet pack for applying heat at home is especially useful when you are unable to take hot tub baths. It is effective in relaxing muscles and in relieving mild discomfort. The full wet pack is used when your aches and pains are not too severe. You will also find this particular method desirable for preparing your body for massage.

You will not be able to apply the full wet pack yourself. Your home care assistant will have to do it for you. However, no special equipment or training is necessary. The only materials you need are a warm room with the temperature at 72 degrees F., a bed-sized piece of rubber sheeting, an old blanket, a full-sized

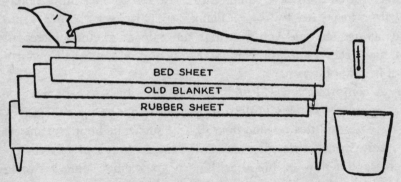

BED SHEET
OLD BLANKET
RUBBER SHEET

Full Wet Pack applied (top), and materials needed (below).

bed sheet, a large bucket of water at 110 degrees F., and a bed.

Spread the rubber sheeting over the entire bed and the blanket on top of it. Lie down on your back, completely nude, on top of the blanket and in the center of the bed. The bed sheet should be folded lengthwise in wide pleat-like folds so that it will be possible to quickly tuck it under and around you.

The person applying the full wet pack dips the sheet into the hot water and wrings it out. The sheet is then spread quickly under you. Raise your arms over your head. Your home care assistant will wrap one-half of the wet sheet about you. Lower your arms to your sides. The second half of the sheet will then go around you, including your shoulders. The halves of sheeting between your legs will be wrapped individually around each leg right down to your feet.

Your home care assistant should work quickly, making sure that the entire wet sheet is tucked snugly around you. Then, the blanket that is beneath you is brought up and around you and tucked in firmly, especially around your feet and your neck. The only part of you that will be exposed from this snug package is your head. The blanket will insulate your body and make it possible for a layer of warm moist air to collect between your skin and the wet sheet. It may be necessary to toss one or two blankets over you to help maintain the heat. Remain in this position for from 45 to 50 minutes. The full wet-pack treatment should be repeated three or four times during the week.

A word about some other methods

There are a number of common methods for producing heat that have been deliberately omitted from this book. Some of the methods, although beneficial for other purposes, are of little or no value in the treatment of arthritis. Others are impractical and even dangerous for home care use and belong only in the skilled hands of a physician or a trained technician in a hospital or clinic.

You no doubt are wondering, for example, why the nonluminous electric coil heater found in so many homes is not included. This type of heater might do all right in warming your bathroom on a cold winter morning, but it is not at all satisfactory in the treatment of arthritis. While it may produce good intense surface heat on the skin, the heat has almost no tissue-penetrating qualities.

Short-wave diathermy may be all right in a hospital or when given by a physician or physiotherapist. Properly given, it produces internal heat that is helpful in some stages of arthritis. However, the portable units that are available for patient home use must of necessity be equipped with safety governors, which reduce their value. Home diathermy can prove valuable, though, when applied by a trained therapist. Used indiscriminately, diathermy can be harmful.

The electric blanket may keep you warm and comfortable on a cold night when the heat in your home is off. But the heat that is produced by the blanket is far from sufficient to be of any therapeutic value. Recently electric mittens have been introduced as a more pleasant substitute for the paraffin bath. The mittens, which are nothing more than heating pads shaped into gloves, provide good low-grade heat and can be safely worn night or day. They have, though, limited use.

Among the heat-producing devices that have no place at all in the treatment of arthritis at home are: lamps that emit ultraviolet rays; machines that produce faradic, galvanic, and sinusoidal electrical currents; and gadgets that produce and sustain high fevers. In the hands of an inexperienced person these may even prove to be dangerous and harmful. The best forms of heat care for home care use in arthritis are those described in this chapter.

REMEMBER THESE POINTS
ABOUT HEAT

✔ 1. Heat, correctly applied, lessens pain, and prepares you for massage and exercise. (Both of these procedures are detailed in the next chapters.)

✔ 2. There are many ways of applying heat. It's important that you use the one best suited to your particular problem. Check with your doctor about this.

✔ 3. You don't need to spend a lot of money to get the heating apparatus described in this chapter. Simple instructions are given for building them at little or no expense.

✔ 4. About half these heating methods require no apparatus beyond materials commonly found in the home.

~~~ **5**

MASSAGE AS
AN AID IN
ARTHRITIS TREATMENT

Nothing can substitute for the skill and the control that are contained in a pair of human hands.

But there is more to massage than the mere rubbing or the patting of a joint. Massage is a medical art that is based on scientifically accurate principles. It is a definite form of treatment that may even be said to be a cornerstone of modern physical therapy. It is one of the most useful methods for overcoming arthritic misery, one that will never be effectively replaced. Mechanical massagers and vibrators now on the market are of no value in arthritis and many have even proved harmful.

Massage stimulates and relaxes

Properly applied, massage has two beneficial effects. There is the *mechanical* effect—the action that pumps and milks—which improves the nourishing circulation of your blood lymph, the fluid that bathes your tissues. This action also helps remove irritating waste matter that accumulates around an arthritic joint, adding to the inflammation and swelling. What is more, the mechanical effect softens and stretches your tightened muscles and tendons, thus adding to your joint's range of motion.

Then there is the *reflex* effect of massage, that which helps you relax your muscles. Massage induces sedation and so helps ease pain and prevents the formation of motion-restricting adhesions. In this respect, massage is an effective complement to heat therapy.

Massage is never performed unless heat treatments have preceded it. It is heat that will start many of the beneficial processes flowing within a joint, but it is gentle massage that will continue them through the arthritic area.

And according to Dr. Edward B. McLean, arthritis specialist of California, "Massage, when applied with discrimination, appears to afford considerable relief of symptoms and may hasten recovery of the affected joints."

How your assistant begins

There is a definite technique to massage, especially as it is used in arthritis. Properly used, massage will improve muscle tone and restore normal motion. Not applied correctly, it may aggravate your joints and even contribute to further damage. *For example, the beating, slapping, and kneading techniques commonly employed in health parlors and Turkish or Swedish baths have no place in arthritis.*

There are several techniques used in the application of massage. Not all can be utilized in every stage of arthritis. Each has its own definite purpose and is aimed at bringing about a very particular response within the painful and swollen arthritic joint. Because of this, it is important that massage be prescribed by your doctor and that the initial treatments be given by a skilled masseur who is also familiar with the problems of arthritis. Once the pattern of massage is set, the necessary procedures can be taught your home care assistant.

The basic techniques are simple

Of the numerous techniques of massage, there are two that are the most useful in arthritis. These two also happen to be the simplest of all massage procedures and the ones that are the most practical for home care use. The first is *stroking* and the other is *friction*. Let's take a closer look at both of these.

There is more to stroking than the name implies. Stroking in massage follows a very definite pattern. *The strokes are long and smooth and always around the joint and toward the heart.* Stroking gently toward the heart encourages the stagnant venous blood to return for refreshing and relaying into the circulatory system. In a joint that has been inactive for some time, the throbbing action of the muscles usually is at a low ebb. As a result, some of the used blood is slow in leaving the veins in the diseased area.

Friction massage uses the ends of the fingers to reactivate deep tissues in a joint area. Friction is accomplished by circular motions transmitted through the massager's rigidly held fingers. As the finger tips move in small circles against the surface of the body, the underlying soft tissues move with the action. This particular technique is often of value when performed in the immediate vicinity of an involved joint. Friction, useful in itself, is most effective when done with stroking.

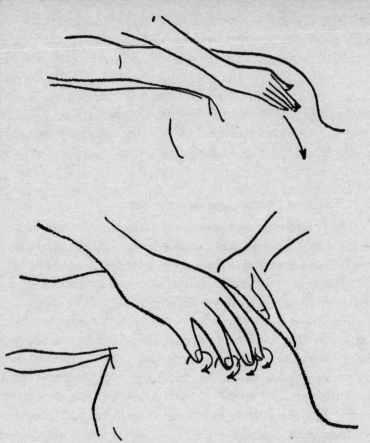

The Stroking technique (top), the Friction technique (below).

When not to use massage

Useful as it is, not everyone is able to enjoy the benefits of massage. For example, it should never be used during the acute stage of arthritis when even the mildest stroking may aggravate the disease and add to your pain and misery. Neither should massage be applied when an involved joint is hot and throbbing and obviously highly inflamed or when your body temperature is above 100 degrees F. You should also avoid massage if after the initial treatment you find that the pain, swelling, or stiffness in your affected joint has increased. If after an hour or two following massage the discomfort has not subsided, then the chances are you are not as yet ready for massage.

There are a number of other instances when massage should not be used, or for that matter, even attempted. Get your doctor to determine whether, in particular situations, massage may or may not be advisable. For example, you should never attempt massage if you are suffering from *phlebitis*, the inflammation of a vein. And there is the danger of *embolism*, a sudden blocking of a blood vessel by a clot or some other obstruction that the massage has forced into place. Massage also is not advisable if you suffer from certain skin disorders or if you suffer from hypetension, hardening of the arteries, or certain bone diseases.

(Massage is most effective, in chronic arthritis, when the disease has settled down to a steady and persistent pace. When the highly inflammatory process has subsided, the tissues surrounding the involved joint are for the first time able to tolerate even the mildest techniques of massage. So as not to lose any of the benefits that come from massage, it should be started as soon as the joints have quieted down.)

The bedridden may use a milder form

Your doctor may see fit to prescribe a mild routine of massage during the early stages of the disease, especially when extended bed rest is involved. Although the gentle techniques he may recommend may cause some minor discomfort, his principal concern will be to offset the threat of adhesions and the quick weakening of muscles associated with the diseased joint. In these instances, massage will be directed not at the inflamed joint itself but at the muscles and the tissues that surround it.

For example, if the knees are involved, massage will be directed at the thighs and the lower legs.

Getting yourself ready

When massage is applied, great care should be taken that there is no draft in the room. The temperature in the room should be about 70 degress F. You should be lying down fully relaxed. This not only makes it easier to apply massage, but it also eliminates the pull of gravity from the affected joint and helps the circulation. Remove all clothing from the area to be massaged. It may even be better if you remove all your outer garments, cover yourself with a light blanket, and leave the area to be massaged exposed.

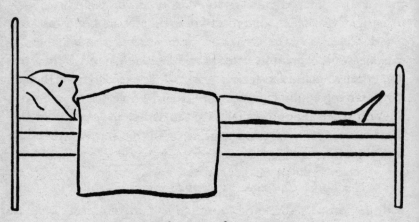

Expose the area for massage.

Too little is better than too much

When it is first used, massage is never applied for more than five minutes at a time. Gradually, this may be increased to 10 and then to 15 minutes. At no time, however, should a massage treatment last more than 15 minutes in any one location on the body. Usually, five to 10 minutes is allotted for an arm, 10 minutes for a leg, and from 10 to 15 minutes for the back. Unless your doctor advises otherwise, two massage sessions a day, each to follow a heat treatment, will be sufficient. *One thing to remember is that it is always safer to give too little massage than too much.* The overuse of massage may, if you are not careful, undo the progress brought about by other means of therapy.

Begin with light strokes

Regardless of what form of massage has been prescribed, each treatment is begun with very light stroking. All massage strokes must be slow and uniform. There never should be enough pressure to produce pain. At the outset, each stroke is exceedingly light, almost to a point of being superficial. The hands are passed delicately over the skin in a slightly circular direction. Their smooth rhythmic strokes should not exceed 15 a minute. After a while, the strokes are gradually emphasized though still retaining their gentleness and their rhythm.

With succeeding treatments deeper strokes may be attempted in an effort to affect the underlying tissues and muscles. Even though the strokes may cover a considerable area, the deep pressure that is brought to bear is but for a moment, the force for that instant being straight down. The pressure is applied with the palm of the hand; the thumbs and fingers are used to mold the natural form of the area being massaged. It is this action that will squeeze and stretch the muscles and empty the involved lymph and blood vessels. As the person giving you massage becomes more experienced, his sense of touch will guide him in the amount of pressure to use and in the amount of time to allow between strokes so as to permit the blood vessels to empty.

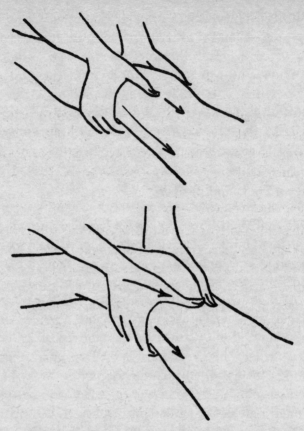

The palms apply the pressure; the fingers follow the natural contours.

THE STROKING TECHNIQUE

The stroking motion is perhaps the most desirable technique to use in arthritis. It is gentle and it can be adjusted in keeping with the soreness of the involved joint. All stroking motions are long and smooth and are executed in one direction only, toward the heart, never back and forth. Each stroke is like an airplane gliding in for a landing, only to take off again after making contact with the ground. Stroking is begun at that part of the limb that is attached to the body. This is to empty the superficial veins and the lymph vessels. Gradually, the strokes are lengthened to include the entire section of the limb.

When your arm, for example, is to be massaged, the stroking action is started at the elbow. Each stroke is directed toward the shoulder—in other words, toward the heart. Gradually, the strokes are lengthened to include the shoulder area. After several minutes, the originating point moves from the elbow down to the wrist. Stroking now begins at the wrist and extends up to the elbow, then from the elbow up to the shoulder. Finally, the strokes are begun at the finger tips and are worked up to the wrist, with the wrist-to-elbow and elbow-to-shoulder stroking following.

In massaging your leg, a similar pattern is followed. This time, massage is started at the knee and the strokes are directed toward the hip—again, toward the heart. This action, like that for the upper arm, is designed to open the various blood and lymph vessels that lead to the heart. As stroking continues, the person applying massage moves the starting point from the knee to the ankle and finally from the ankle to the toes. Each time an additional section of the leg is included, the strokes are

First, the upper arm and shoulder, then the whole arm (stroke is interrupted at the elbow).

extended to take in the previously massaged section. In the last five minutes of massage, the entire extremity from the toes to the hip or from the fingers to the shoulder is covered.

Stroke begins above knee and gradually includes lower leg and foot.

THE FRICTION TECHNIQUE

There are times when the friction technique of massage is a useful follow-up to stroking. For that matter, friction is seldom used unless stroking has been applied first. In the very nature of its execution, friction is a confining and limited technique. Friction is most effective in a single problem area. For example, it is often used around a knee joint or at the shoulder or ankle. It is also quite effective when applied to the back of the neck and the base of the spine.

Friction consists of small circular movements made by the fingers of the person giving the treatment. No other parts of this individual's hand but the tips of the fingers come in contact with your body. One or more fingers may be used at a time and the action generally is concentrated in but a small area. Friction may be applied with one hand, but often two hands are used simultaneously, each performing the same procedure but on two sides of the same joint.

The small circular movements of the finger tips, when combined with deep pressure, move the underlying soft tissues. There may be some discomfort and so too much force should be avoided. If friction causes pain or results in muscle soreness, it should not be repeated. Friction isn't too easy a technique to master and as a result it is not prescribed too frequently. When properly applied, it can be highly effective. However, should your home care assistant be unable to do it, stroking motions alone will be quite sufficient.

There are several pointers that you and the person who will do your massage should keep in mind, if the massage is to be at all effective. Massage is primarily a procedure for muscles and surrounding tissue. It is very seldom that joints are subjected to direct massage, especially when they are inflamed. No pressure is ever placed upon the bony projection of a joint. All stroking and friction that involve a joint move around it rather than over it. To reduce skin friction, such lubricants as cocoa butter, mineral oil, or talcum powder may be used.

It is essential that you be comfortable and completely relaxed

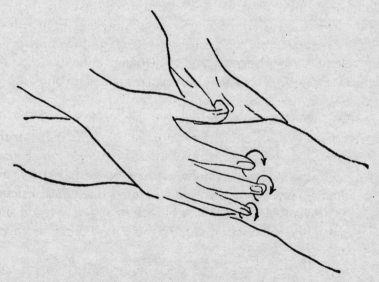

Only the tips of the fingers are used in friction massage.

throughout each treatment. All massage should be applied only when you are lying down, even if only your fingers are being treated. Sitting or reclining, no matter how comfortable you may be, will produce general body muscle tension and fatigue and so counteract the efforts of the massager. Remaining quiet and at rest after each session, even snoozing or sleeping for 30 or 45 minutes or so, will permit you to prolong the benefits of massage and thus aid your recovery even more. It is also important that your doctor check your progress regularly so that the massage may be modified in accordance with your improvement.

Dr. Bowie has said of this phase of home care: "Massage is one of the most useful, easily obtained, and frequently neglected methods of therapy in arthritis." Don't you neglect massage. Remember that there is a soothing art in a pair of hands.

REMEMBER THESE POINTS ABOUT MASSAGE

✔ 1. Massage has two good effects. FIRST, it improves circulation of the blood while removing the irritating waste matter that accumulates around an arthritic joint. SECOND, it induces *sedation,* that is, it relieves pain and helps make movement freer and more comfortable.

✔ 2. There is more to massage than simple rubbing or patting. It is scientific therapy. But a relative or friend of yours can learn the techniques and apply them daily at home.

✔ 3. Mechanical massagers or vibrators are of NO value in arthritis. They could even be harmful.

(pages 94-96 combined on this page)

SPECIAL EXERCISE CAN MAKE YOU INDEPENDENT

IT DOESN'T MATTER WHAT FORM OF ARTHRITIS YOU HAVE or what the course of your treatment has been. Eventually, you will have to turn to exercise if you are to prevent crippling and preserve the function of your arthritic joints. Properly selected exercise will rapidly restore the lost motion and the lost strength and power to your stiffened and weakened joints.

Exercise is not physical exertion

Exercise for you, the arthritic, is not the physical exertion that comes with the playing of a set of tennis or a round of golf. Nor is it the excessive joint activity that comes with walking ten blocks to work or riding a bicycle around the park each morning. Moving about as you do at your job or at home, if you are a homemaker, isn't exercise either. *One of the gravest mistakes you can make is to try to work your arthritis out of your joints by being continually active.*

Exercise in arthritis is quite the opposite of the commonly accepted definition of the word. *Exercise in arthritis actually avoids physical exertion and overactivity on the part of your joints.* Instead, it is a definite therapeutic procedure aimed at one particular group of muscles at a time. It is a specialized routine that maintains a joint's normal range of motion and increases it, if it has been restricted, but without harming it any further. Without strong muscles, good bone position within a joint cannot be maintained.

Heat and massage come first

There are at least five different forms of therapeutic exercise used in arthritis. The form you use will depend a great deal upon your particular problem. It will also depend upon the kind of arthritis you have, the stage it is at, and the progress you are making with whatever other treatments you are getting. *No matter what type of exercise you use, it will always follow the application of heat and massage. For it is heat and massage that make therapeutic exercise possible.*

Active exercise without help

Early in the disease when motion in your joints is still quite free and easy, the chances are you will be put on a routine of active exercise. Here, all movement will be done by you without any resistance or assistance. The various exercises will involve the movement of your joints against gravity, or else with gravity reduced to a minimum—that is, by the use of a sling or by doing the exercises on a smooth-surfaced board or even in a tub of water. *Active exercises* are directed at groups of muscles that need strengthening or retraining. Performed slowly, they carry a joint through the full range of motion making complete use of the involved muscles.

Active exercise with help

When there is a moderate limitation of motion and perhaps even considerable muscular weakness, *active assistive* exercises— that is, exercises done with the help of your assistant—will be prescribed. While these particular exercises are basically *active*, your home care assistant or some mechanical device will be necessary to assist you. Sometimes, all the assistance you will need will be an initial nudge or push to start the movement of your joint, with you following through and completing the exercise. It may also be necessary for the person helping you to guide the action of your joint and even to apply gentle force or stretching to complete the full range of motion.

A mechanical device you may be able to use is the overhead pulley. The overhead pulley consists of a single one-inch pulley suspended from a hook in the center of a door jamb. A six-foot length of clothesline is passed through the pulley and the ends tied in loops to form hand grips. The device can be used either in a sitting or a standing position. You exercise by holding the looped ends of the line, using one arm to pull up the other and alternating the pull in a see-saw fashion.

The development and maintenance of muscular strength may call for the use of a carefully performed series of *active resistance* exercise. The resistance may be manual, in that the home care assistant resists your effort to move your joint. It may also be progressive, in which case weights such as leaded boots and sandbags are attached to the involved limb during the exercise. Care must be taken in using these particular exercises in chronic arthritis because of the pain and the harm they may cause an inflamed joint. However, when performed gently without the intent of increasing muscle power rapidly, this form of exercise can be quite useful.

Two exercises for the bedridden

If you happen to be confined to bed or are spending much of your time in a chair because rest for the moment is more important than activity, there are still two useful forms of exercise for you.

First, there is *passive exercise* during which you do nothing but relax and permit your home care assistant to move your joint for you. Passive exercise, though taking your joint through its normal range of motion, does not require the exertion of muscle power.

Second, there is *static* or *muscle-setting exercise* during which you develop the knack of contracting your muscles while lying perfectly still and not even moving your joints. Static exercise, which should be done about four times a day, helps prevent the weakening and the deterioration of essential muscles, especially those necessary for walking, climbing stairs, and getting in and out of chairs.

A little each day is best

Exercise should be performed judiciously. A slow gradual course with a little done each day is far more effective than an aggressive daily routine. Besides, slow motions will produce the least discomfort. Rapid and jerky movements will result in a tired and stiffened joint in addition to the problem that already exists. Remember, when you are exercising an arthritic joint you are not seeking to develop a set of bulging muscles.

The right routine is important

One aim in carefully selecting a course of exercise is to avoid pain. Though some pain and stiffness should be expected when exercise is first begun and often when it is actually being performed, no exercise should be continued if it produces prolonged pain. First, try to reduce the exercise. If this does not help, discontinue it altogether. You should also stop using any exercise that brings on a tremor in your involved muscles or a tightening feeling in the joint itself. Should any ache or pain develop after you have exercised and then continue for several hours, it is an indication that you have either exercised too much or that you have done the exercise too quickly. If the discomfort increases, it may be that the particular routine has been too severe for you and that it should be revised or modified.

Because of their simplicity and because of the monotony connected with all exercises, many that are used in the treatment of arthritis are often not fully appreciated. Many a person after trying a particular routine for several days will abandon the exercise and decide it is not worth the bother. This is especially true in the early stages of arthritis when the stricken joint is still moveable and the purpose of the exercise is *prevention rather than correction.* You cannot overlook the fact that it is far easier to prevent a deformity than to try to reverse it. *Besides, the more preventive exercise you do, the less need will there be for corrective exercise.* Preventive exercise should therefore become as much of a habit with you as brushing your teeth.

Exercises will work if you will

Speaking of therapeutic exercise, Dr. Bowie called it "the only means by which the bulk and strength of muscles may be increased. Exercises help prevent muscular atrophy and in some instances, decalcification of bone."

Should exercise fail either to prevent deformity or to correct limitations of joint function, the chances are that the fault is basically with you. Even the most skillfully selected routine may fail simply because you have not exercised properly. Your exercise periods were either too short or too infrequent, thus not permitting the procedure to make any lasting impression upon your arthritic joint or its surrounding muscles. Not taking your exercises seriously, and attempting to cut corners in performing the selected routines, are other reasons for failing to benefit from this extremely valuable form of physical therapy.

It goes without saying that exercises that have not been properly prescribed and those that have not been properly supervised will also fail to achieve the desired results. Frequent review of your exercises by your doctor will assure that the routines you are doing are in keeping with your needs. As your condition improves and as joint function increases, many exercises will have to be changed.

No matter how much improvement your joint may show, it is not wise to exercise for more than one-half hour at a time. Overdoing any exercise may do you more harm than good. Neither is it wise to deviate from the prescribed routines or to improvise your own forms of exercise without the knowledge of your doctor. For to be at all effective, the exercises you do must be selected for you, the best being those that will give you a good range of motion in your involved joint. So that you will remember to do your exercises, make them a part of your daily routine—for example, preceding your meals. Remember too that every period of exercise should be followed by an equal period of rest.

Set up a schedule

Do not overexert yourself when you exercise. The good that you accomplish will come from the cumulative effect at the end of a day and not from any single period of exercise. Each full course of exercise should be repeated at four different intervals during the day. A reasonable daily schedule is to exercise at 8

A.M., 12 Noon, 4 P.M. and 8 P.M., with the first three sessions taking place before meals. This particular schedule will permit you to rest between sessions and also to make proper and sufficient use of heat and massage before each period of exercise. Whatever schedule you adopt, keep it the same every day, seven days a week.

Lie down and start gently

You will note that most of the following exercises are to be done while lying down in bed. There is a good reason for this. First, you will find it much easier to exercise in this position. Not only will your body be relaxed and at rest, but you will not be fighting the pull of gravity on the very joints you are trying to help. A reclining position also permits your body to undergo its full range of breathing, thus giving you a more active circulation of blood and body fluids. As you improve, you will find that you will be able to do many of the exercises in a standing position.

If your joints are severely involved, start each exercise period with a brief session of passive routines. Let your home care assistant help your joint through several simple and gentle motions. A most effective warm-up is to ease your involved joint through its normal movements. This not only will help prepare the arthritic joint for the more active exercise that is to follow, but it will also give you a fairly good idea of the limitations of motion that may exist. What is more, it will also vividly dramatize the vast difference between normal activity of a joint and the more specific action of therapeutic exercise.

The following exercises are grouped according to the various joints and limbs and sections of the body that may be affected. All of these exercises were carefully selected by arthritis specialists. Your doctor should check off those particularly suited for you. None of them should hurt you when done in moderation but some may do you more good than others, all depending on the activity of the disease.

Except where it is otherwise specified, you should do each of your exercises three to five times. As your muscles become stronger and as your range of joint motion improves, you should increase this to 10 to 20 times. This, however, is not to be taken as a definitely required prescription. Your own energy should be a guide to the number of times you do an exercise. *You must never do any exercise long enough to tire you or to cause you undue fatigue.*

EXERCISES FOR YOUR HAND AND WRIST

Normal movement for passive exercise

Move your hand forward, then backward, as if you were waving good-bye to someone. Repeat several times. Then, have your home care assistant gently rotate your hand, moving it first to the left and then to the right as if you were shooing flies off a food dish.

Active exercises

• 1. Make a tight fist, closing all your fingers and thumb. Hold for a moment. Open your hand fully and repeat.

• 2. Stand against a table, facing it. Hold your hand out, stretching your fingers as straight as you can. While your fingers are in this position, place your hand, palm down, on the table top. With your hand in this position, firmly place your other hand down on the hand being exercised. Now, raise the forearm and elbow of the involved arm slowly, at the same time trying to flatten the bent fingers of your arthritic hand. Lower your forearm and repeat.

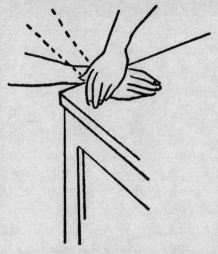

A simple massage for hand and wrist. (Exercise 2.)

• 3. Grip a doorknob with your hand and turn it back and forth. In time, as strength returns to your hand and wrist, ask your home care assistant to offer some resistance by holding the knob on the other side of the door while you exercise.

• 4. Hold a short rod or a length of broomstick in your hand. Keep your elbow still and close to your hip. Rotate your wrist, first to the right and then to the left in a door-knob action.

• 5. Keep your hand extended, palm down and fingers close together. Spread your fingers apart, then close them and repeat several times.

• 6. Hold your hand in front of your face, the palm toward you. Slowly bring the tip of each finger over, one at a time, to touch the tip of your thumb. As you bring each finger over, make as perfect an arc as you can. Repeat, this time touching the tips of your fingers to the cheek of your palm at the base of the thumb. Alternate between the two routines.

• 7. Shake your hand as if you were trying to cool it. Repeat this several times between exercises.

• 8. Hold your hand up as if you were stopping traffic. Move your hand first toward your thumb and then toward your little finger in the motion of an automobile windshield wiper.

• 9. Grasp the fingers of your hand and pull them gently. Gradually increase the pull. At first, grasp and pull all your fingers at once. Then, repeat, pulling one finger at a time. If both your hands are involved, let your home care assistant help you.

• 10. Extend both your arms in front of you, palms together. Keeping your elbow extended as much as possible, sharply bring your right forearm toward your chest so that your thumb will strike your chest just beneath your chin. Keep the left hand extended. Bring your right forearm out again. When the palms of your hands touch, bring your left forearm in toward your chest, keeping your right extended. Alternate several times.

• 11. Assume the same position as above, your forearms extended in front of you, the palms of your hands touching. This time, keep your palms together and bring your forearms in toward the chest so that your hands assume an attitude of prayer. Your elbows are extended outwardly. Keeping your palms together, extend your arms to the starting position and repeat.

• 12. Face the wall and place the palm of your hand against the wall at about shoulder level. Your elbow should be slightly bent and the fingers of your hand should be pointing upward. Keeping your fingers straight, slowly slide your hand down the wall as far as it will go. Slide your hand slowly up to the starting position and repeat.

EXERCISES FOR YOUR FINGERS

Normal movement for passive exercise

Have your home care assistant gently bend your fingers so that their tips touch the palm of your hand. Straighten, and repeat. Your assistant may also try bending your thumb to the center of your palm, keeping the thumb as close to the hand as possible. Straighten your thumb and repeat.

Active exercises

• 1. Keep your fingers straight and together. Bend your hand at the knuckles. Straighten your hand and repeat.

• 2. Bring your thumb and forefinger together in the shape of the letter "o." Straighten your fingers and repeat.

• 3. Put your hand flat on a table, palm down. Raise and lower your fingers, one finger at a time.

• 4. Pick up a sheet of newspaper with your affected hand and then, without any assistance from your other hand, slowly crumple the sheet into a small ball.

Crumpling a newspaper will exercise your fingers. (Exercise 4.)

• 5. Pick up a small rubber ball with your hand. Squeeze the ball as hard as you can. Relax your grip and repeat. If at first the ball offers too much resistance, perform the same exercise with a sponge.

• 6. Perform exercises Nos. 5 and 6 listed under active exercises for hand and wrist.

EXERCISES FOR YOUR FOREARM

Normal movement for passive exercise

With your elbows snugly at your sides, lift your forearms in front of you, palms up. Then, with your forearms in this position, turn palms down. Continue, turning your palms up and down several times.

Active exercises

• 1. Assume the position described above for normal movement of the forearms during passive exercise. This time, make certain that your wrists and your fingers are extended as straight as possible. Then, smartly twist your forearms, alternating from a palms-up to a palms-down position.

• 2. While in bed, rest your forearms on the bed with your hands over the edge, palms down. Keep your fingers fully extended. Raise your hands up, then bend them down, keeping your forearms on the bed.

• 3. Assume the same position as described in No. 2 above but with your palms up. This time keep twisting your wrists back and forth as if you were turning a door knob.

• 4. Assume the position as described in No. 3 above. With a very smart and snappy beat, close your hand into a fist and open it again, straightening your fingers as much as possible.

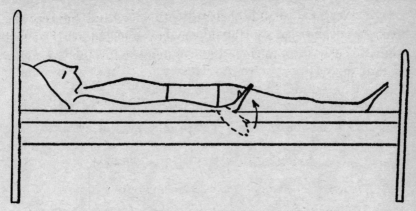

A good exercise for the forearm. (Exercise 2.)

EXERCISES FOR YOUR ELBOW

Normal movement for passive exercise

Stand in a relaxed position. With your elbow at your side, slowly bend your forearm upwards until the tips of your fingers touch the shoulder of the same arm. Bring your arm down gently and repeat.

Active exercises

• 1. Lie down, your hands at your sides, palms up and elbows resting on the bed. Bring the fingers of your involved hand to the top of that hand's shoulder. Bring your hand slowly down to the bed, straightening your elbow and keeping the palms of your hand up.

• 2. Stand facing a table. Place your hand on the table, palm down. Slowly lean forward over the table, bending your elbow as you move your body downward and straightening your elbow as you return to the starting position. Repeat without removing your hand from the table.

• 3. Face a wall, standing about two feet from it. Place your hands flat against the wall, shoulder high. Keeping your feet in position, push the upper part of your body toward the wall, bending your elbows as you move forward. Touch your shoulders to your hands. Push your body back to the starting position, straightening your elbows as you go back. May be done with both hands on the wall or with one hand at a time.

Stand about two feet from the wall. (Exercise 3.)

EXERCISES FOR YOUR SHOULDER

Normal movement for passive exercise

Stand at attention. Raise your arm forward and upward over your head. Return the arm to your side by reversing this movement. From the same position, raise your arm sideways, past shoulder level and then upwards over your head. Follow the same path in bringing your arm down to your side. May be done simultaneously with both arms for better body balance.

Active exercises

• 1. In a standing position, shrug your shoulders—first upward and downward, and then in a circular motion. May also be done while seated upright in bed.

• 2. Stand erect alongside a wall with your shoulder nearest it. Bring your arm up and out to shoulder level, the fingers barely touching the wall. From this position, slowly start to climb the wall with your fingers. Take small "steps" using your index and middle fingers. At first you may not be able to climb more than two or three "steps." As you progress the number will increase.

• 3. Assume a position that is halfway between erect and a stoop. Let your arms dangle freely toward the ground. Slowly

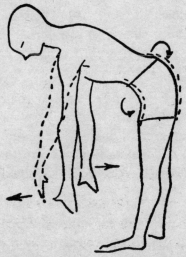

**Let your arms swing freely.
(Exercise 3.)**

rock your body back and forth at the hips until both arms start to swing. Let your arms swing back and forth as if they were walking.

• 4. Stand erect as if you were preparing to dive into a pool. Swing your arms forward and upward over your head. Bring them down in the same sweeping motion, letting them continue their swing backward.

• 5. Stand erect. Raise your arms sidewards and upwards, clapping your hands over your head. Bring your arms down again with the same sweeping motion. Repeat, but this time instead of clapping your palms together, bring the backs of your hands together. Alternate from one to the other.

• 6. Stand erect. Keep your hands at your sides, your elbows and your wrists stiff. Make a circular motion with your arm, increasing the size of the circle until the swing brings your arm practically to shoulder level. Exercise one arm at a time.

• 7. Lie face down on your bed. Clasp your hands behind your neck. Raise both elbows and your head from the bed. Do not raise or lift your body. Return to the starting position and repeat.

• 8. Sit upright, either in bed or in a chair. Fold your arms in front of you, Indian fashion, keeping your elbows shoulder high. Unfold your arms, bringing them out and your elbows sharply back, still at shoulder level. Return to the original position and repeat, keeping your elbows shoulder high at all times.

EXERCISES FOR YOUR NECK

Normal movements for passive exercise

Assume a relaxed standing or sitting position. Bend your head slowly forward. Then, bring it back, keeping your chin in as much as possible. Bend your head to the left, straighten, and then bend it to the right. Straighten, and repeat. Turn your head so you face your left shoulder, face forward, and then turn your head so you face your right shoulder. Face forward, and repeat.

Active exercises

• 1. Lie flat on your back across the width of your bed with your head hanging over the edge. Tighten your neck muscles and bring your head slowly up until your chin touches your chest. Let your head drop slowly back. Relax for a moment and repeat.

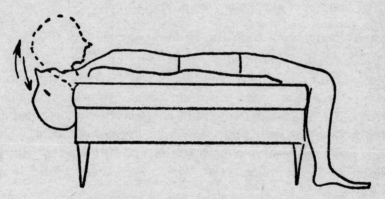

Raise and lower your head slowly. (Exercise 1.)

• 2. Assume the same position as for No. 1 above. Again tighten your neck muscles, but this time turn your head slowly to the left. Straighten your head and then turn it to the right. Straighten, and repeat.

• 3. Assume the same position as for Nos. 1 and 2 above. Put your hands behind your head, locking your fingers tightly. Keep your elbows back. With your hands, slowly push your head forward while at the same time resisting this effort with your neck.

After bringing your head as far forward as you can, slowly begin pushing it back to the starting position, this time resisting the effort with your clasped hands. Relax a moment and repeat.

• 4. Assume a relaxed sitting or standing position. Turn your head to the right. Then, slowly raise your head and rotate it to the left as if you were following an airplane in flight. Bring your head slowly down and rotate it back to the right, and repeat. When doing this circular rotation of your neck, you may imagine your chin inscribing a circle on a blackboard in front of your face.

EXERCISES FOR YOUR HIPS

Normal movements for passive exercise

While seated in bed in a relaxed position, have your home care assistant slowly move your hip for you. Have your leg moved out to the side as far as it will go, keeping your knees straight and your toe pointed straight ahead. Have the leg returned to the starting position. While seated at the edge of the bed with your legs hanging down, have the involved leg moved behind the other. As your legs cross, rotate your affected thigh outwardly.

Active exercises

• 1. Lie on your back, keeping your legs perfectly straight. Slowly slide your legs apart as far as they will go. Return to the starting position, and repeat.

• 2. Assume the same position that you did in No. 1 above. This time slowly raise and lower your leg, keeping your knee straight. After several turns, repeat this movement bending your knee somewhat. Alternate between both procedures.

• 3. Assume the same position that you did in Nos. 1 and 2. Bend your knee and grasp it with both your hands. Slowly force your knee up against your chest as far as it will go. Return to the starting position, and repeat.

• 4. Stand at right angles to a table, about a foot away, with your good hip nearest the table. Shift your weight to your good leg, at the same time resting your buttock against the table. This will lift your arthritic leg off the floor. While in this position swing your leg back and forth from your affected hip.

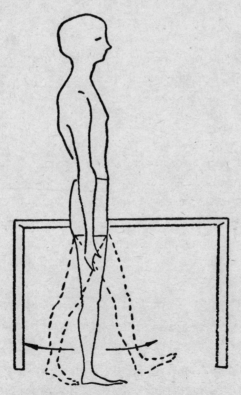

**Swing your leg from the hip.
(Exercise 4.)**

• 5. Stand at attention. Bend forward and touch your toes without bending your knees. Return to upright position, and repeat.

• 6. Lie flat on your back, your legs perfectly straight. Tighten the muscles of your thigh. Relax, and repeat. This particular exercise is designed especially for bed patients. If you are confined to bed, repeat this exercise from five to ten times every hour.

EXERCISES FOR YOUR KNEES

Normal movements for passive exercise

Though the knee can be put through its normal paces from a seated position, you will find it much easier to do so while resting in bed on your back. Lying down also will allow your knee joint and its intricate pattern of muscles and tendons to completely relax. While in this position, have your home care assistant bend your knee as far as it will possibly go. Straighten your leg and repeat.

Active exercises

• 1. Lie flat on your back. Keep your legs straight. Contract the muscles of your entire leg, tightening and straightening your knee cap. Flatten the back of your knee firmly against the bed.

• 2. Sit up in bed with your legs held straight in front of you. Slowly raise your knee off the bed, at the same time sliding your foot back as far as it will go. Straighten your leg, and repeat.

• 3. Lie flat on your back. Lift your legs high, at the same time putting your hands beneath your hips, propping your body up. Using a steady rhythm, put your legs through bicycling motions.

• 4. Sit with your legs hanging over the edge of your bed. Slowly raise and lower your legs, one at a time. Try to keep a steady pace as you alternate. Your doctor may prescribe the use of sandbags attached to your feet for this particular exercise.

• 5. Lie flat on your stomach. Lift your leg, bending your knee as far as it will go. After a few tries, let your home care assistant help you bend your knee further. You may also loop a scarf around the ankle and, with your hands grasping the ends of the scarf, pull your leg back.

• 6. Kneel on one knee, your good one, your other foot remaining flat on the ground with the arthritic knee bent. Move forward over the raised knee as far as you can. Relax, and repeat.

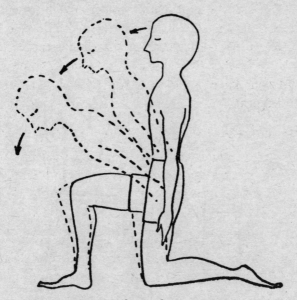

Move forward, as far as you can, then back. (Exercise 6.)

EXERCISES FOR YOUR ANKLE

Normal movements for passive exercise

While seated in bed with your legs hanging over the edge, bend your foot up and down. After several counts, turn your foot in and then out. Alternate between both these motions.

Active exercises

• 1. Sit at the edge of your bed, your feet hanging down toward the floor. Make a circling motion with your affected foot.

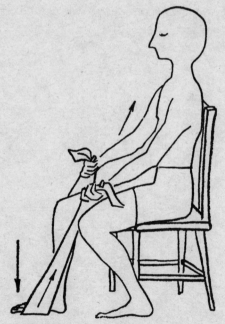

This exercise can be done sitting in a chair, on the edge of your bed, or while lying down. (Exercise 4.)

• 2. Stand at attention, your feet parallel about four inches apart. Slowly rise to your toes, at the same time swinging your heels outward. Return to the starting position, and repeat.

• 3. Stand and face the wall, a little more than arm's-length away. Keep your arms outstretched. Lean forward resting your hands on the wall at shoulder level. Keep your knees straight and your heels flat on the ground. Push yourself back to the starting position, and repeat.

• 4. This exercise can be done while seated in a chair, or at the edge of your bed with your legs hanging over the side, or while in bed with your legs straight in front of you. Loop a strong scarf over the ball of your arthritic foot just back of the toes, gripping the free ends of the scarf in each hand. Pull hard on the scarf, forcing your foot back while at the same time re- sisting this effort with your ankle. Keep your toes curled down- ward and your legs straight.

• 5. Assume a relaxed position in a straight-backed chair. Cross your legs at the ankles, pulling them slightly in toward the chair. Only the outer edges of your feet should be touching the floor. While in this position, bend your toes. Straighten your toes, relax, and repeat.

REMEMBER THESE POINTS
ABOUT SPECIAL EXERCISE

✔ 1. Be sure you understand this:
EXERCISE IN ARTHRITIS IS NOT SIMPLY PHYSICAL ACTIVITY.

✔ 2. Special exercises are:
Therapeutic routines that maintain or restore the normal range of motion of your joints, and build strength in weakened muscles.

✔ 3. They are aimed at one group of muscles at a time.

✔ 4. Never use exercise unless you have first applied heat and massage treatment.

✔ 5. Certain of the exercises contained in this chapter will do more good for you than others. To find the right ones, get your doctor's advice.

∿ 7

MORE INDEPENDENCE
WITH A
SELF-HELP DEVICE

IF ARTHRITIS HAS HANDICAPPED YOU PHYSICALLY, THERE *is* something you can do to overcome it.

Thousands of formerly home-bound arthritics are now returning to active and productive lives, though their physical handicaps remain unchanged. For the first time, they are able to resume their independence and lessen their demands upon the good patience of their relatives and friends.

It is all because of the expansion of the idea first expressed with the development of the crutch—the self-help device. Many a simple homemade self-help device is making the difference between an arthritics's remaining an invalid or being a self-sufficient and economically independent individual.

Self-help devices also conserve energy and protect damaged

joints from further destruction, as well as opening up new areas of independence and self-sufficiency.

A self-help device can be almost anything from a hook on the end of a stick with which to zip up a shoe, to a specially designed stainless steel rocker knife with which to cut the toughest meat with no effort at all. A self-help device can be elaborate and as costly as you may want it to be. However, those that you will find most helpful are not only simple to use, but also simple to make in your own home at barely any cost at all. Basically, a self-help device is to assist you in caring for yourself and in getting about and even in holding a job you couldn't otherwise. A self-help device is a short-cut to self-sufficiency.

The self-help devices illustrated in this chapter have been selected for several reasons. First, because they are the most useful in assisting you with the daily necessities of life. Second, because they are simple and inexpensive devices that in most instances you will be able to make for yourself or have someone make for you. The devices as they are listed here are divided into three broad categories: dressing, feeding, and personal hygiene.

DRESSING

The restricted range of motion with which arthritic joints are so often left, makes dressing a difficult self-care problem. If you are having trouble reaching your legs and your feet, then getting into stockings, shoes, underclothing, skirts or trousers may become a chore. If your upper extremities happen to be involved, then getting into a shirt, a blouse, or a dress becomes a most trying experience. Buttons become difficult to handle especially when they are at the side or on the back of a garment.

There is a knack for getting in and out of your clothes despite your limitations of motions. These, however, are a part of functional training and should be taught you in a hospital or in a rehabilitation center. Such techniques, to be of use, must be tailored specifically to you and your difficulty. The purpose of this particular chapter is merely to introduce you to some of the self-help devices connected with your basic needs.

There are a few general hints about clothing, however, that will help make things easier for you. For example, select one-piece, loose garments; they are easier to get in and out of. A loose sport shirt with short sleeves and an open collar is far more practical than the more conventional dress shirt. Buttons should be large and buttonholes loose. All buttons, hooks, and zippers should be in the front where they are easier to get at.

Here are several self-help devices you can make to help you dress.

Putting on socks

Materials—Four pieces of cloth tape, one-half inch in width and two inches in length. Two pieces of doweling, each 21 inches in length. Two small hooks with screw ends of the type used for hanging cups.

Sew two tape loops, each about one inch in length, on each sock. Place loops on opposite sides of sock about two inches below top edge. Fix a hook in one end of each dowel. Hold one stick in each hand, catch hooks in loops of sock, maneuver foot into sock and pull up.

Putting on stockings

Materials—Two pieces of half-inch cloth tape about 48 inches in length. Two corset or girdle garter fasteners.

Sew or attach a garter fastener to one end of each length of tape. Attach garters to opposite sides of stocking top. Drop stocking to the floor, holding onto tapes. Gently maneuver foot into stocking and slowly pull up.

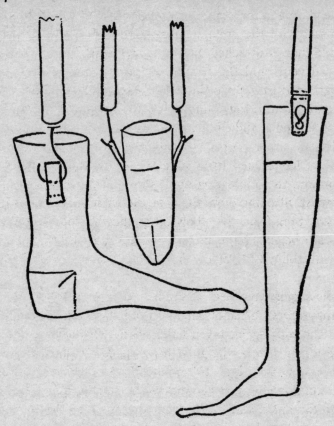

You don't have to bend to put on socks or stockings.

Putting on shoes

Materials—One dowel, 21 inches in length. One small hook with screw end of the type used to hang cups. A metal shoehorn. Two three-inch zippers.

Fix hook into one end of stick; tack and tape shoehorn to the other end. Have shoe repairman sew zippers into shoes. It may be necessary to lengthen shoe opening to make it easier to

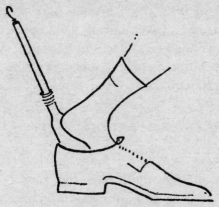

**One end of the dowel is a shoe
horn, the other is a hook for
the zipper.**

slip foot in. With the help of the shoehorn end of the stick,
maneuver shoe into place and foot into shoe. With the hooked
end of the stick zip up the shoe.

Putting on underwear (men and women)

Materials—Two two-inch pieces of half-inch cloth tape. Two
all-purpose 21-inch dowels. Two cup-hanging hooks.

Sew two tape loops on waist band of underwear near each hip.
Screw one hook into end of each stick. Hook sticks into loops.
Open underwear and spread flat on the bed at your feet. While
lying down, insert feet and pull up with sticks. Can also be done
sitting in a chair.

Putting on trousers (same for a skirt)

Materials—Two pieces of half-inch cloth tape, 48 inches in
length. Sturdy pair of ordinary suspenders.

Attach suspenders to trousers in the usual manner. In place
of the suspenders, the tapes can be tied to opposite trouser belt

loops at about the hips. Open trousers and spread them flat on the bed at your feet. Take hold of the suspenders or the ends of cloth tapes. While lying down, insert your feet into the trousers and pull up with either the suspenders or the tapes. Can also be done sitting in a chair.

EATING

Inability to feed yourself can make you feel far more helpless than you really are. Having to have someone spoon-feed you is enough to undermine your morale and jeopardize your efforts to lead a self-sufficient life. Eating can be a real problem when arthritis has settled in your hands and you cannot properly grip your eating utensils, or can do so only with pain. Not helping, either, are the limitations of motion that handicap arms, elbows, and shoulders and make it difficult to bring food to your mouth.

Numerous devices are available commercially that can overcome almost any feeding problem you may experience. For example, knives, spoons, and forks are made with extra-thick plastic handles into which have been grooved the finger impressions of a gripping hand. With the handles being better than an inch in width and in thickness, the utensils can be held by an arthritic hand that cannot close or grip too well. In some instances special handle grips may have to be fashioned. Extensive damage to the wrist and the hand might even make it necessary to angle the handles to conform with the particular degree of limitation.

Ready-made devices are also available commercially to help you bring food to your mouth, despite any restricted motion in your arms, elbows, and shoulders. They usually are made from stainless steel and in effect are nothing more than long-handled eating utensils, usually spoons and forks that are about 11 or 12 inches in length. To cut your food there is a *rocker knife.* The curved blade permits you to cut food with a rocking motion and with a minimum of energy and joint effort; it is especially useful if you are unable to manage two eating utensils at a time. Also available is a long-handled spring clamp to hold a sandwich without mashing it.

Here are a number of self-help devices you or someone else can make to help you feed yourself.

Enlarging the grip on knife, fork, and spoon

Materials—A stainless steel knife, a fork, and a spoon. A sufficient amount of water-base sculpture clay to make three hand-sized handles.

Divide the molding clay into three equal lumps. Knead and shape each lump into a slightly elongated potato, about two by

You can enlarge the handles of eating utensils in various ways.

three inches. Place one of these potatoes across the palm of your hand. Close your fist as far as it will go, squeezing the clay as hard as you can. While holding the lump of clay, have someone insert the handle of the utensil, setting it at the angle most convenient to you. When the clay hardens, the clay handle will be tailored exactly to your grip.

Materials—A stainless steel knife, fork, and spoon with their handles trimmed or shaved down to the width of a spike. Three wooden handles of the type used by carpenters to hold files.

Tap each eating utensil into the hole provided in the end of the wooden handle. The thickness of the handle will provide a comfortable and suitable grip.

Knife in an ordinary carpenter's file handle.

Extending the length of knife, fork, and spoon

Materials—A stainless steel knife, fork, and spoon with handles trimmed or shaved down to the width of a spike. Three half-inch dowels about nine inches in length.

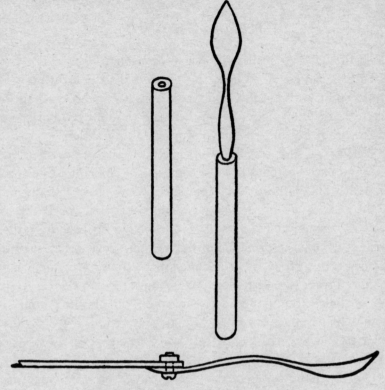

Two ways to give eating utensils a longer handle.

Drill hole into one end of stick and tap in eating utensil. A bit of cement will help keep the utensil snugly set in the dowel.

Materials—A stainless steel knife, fork, and spoon, preferably with flat, unadorned handles. Three strips of stainless steel about the width of the utensil handle and about seven inches in length. Three small bolts and nuts.

Bore hole about one inch from end of utensil handle and a like hole about one inch from end of stainless steel strip. Overlap ends, matching newly bored holes. Insert bolt and nut and tighten.

PERSONAL HYGIENE

To the average healthy individual, personal hygiene is something that can easily be taken for granted. To the arthritic with limited joint motion, just being able to wash, comb the hair, or take care of toilet needs without having to depend upon someone, actually becomes a source of joy and satisfaction.

When motion is restricted in the elbows and the wrists, some commonplace personal tasks become rather difficult to perform properly. They are washing your face, combing your hair, and in the case of a man, shaving. Should your wrists be badly involved, personal cleanliness at a toilet may also become rather difficult. The basic principle of the self-help devices designed to overcome this group of problems is the extension or long handle that brings the wash cloth up to your face and the comb up to your hair without the need of extending or straining your affected joints. There is even available a curved plastic toilet-tissue holder that will permit you to cleanse the otherwise inaccessible parts of your person with little effort.

Though many self-help devices to assist you with your personal hygiene can be made or improvised by you, a number of them will have to be bought. For example, the raised toilet seat. Standard toilets are far too low when motion in the knees and hips is restricted. Available, commercially, are toilet seats with special brackets that slip easily onto the toilet bowl, thus raising the height from four to six inches. Bars and arm rests that fit around the toilet bowl to assist you in getting on and off the seat are also available.

Perhaps the most difficult personal-hygiene problem for most arthritics is tub bathing. Not only does the arthritic find it difficult getting in and out of the tub, but sitting down and then trying to get up again can often be practically impossible.

A walk-in stall shower level with the floor would of course simplify matters a great deal. But with the bathtub being a fairly standard fixture in most homes, a large selection of self-help devices has become available, commercially, to help you bathe without too much difficulty. Examples are aluminum folding steps to get you up, over, and into a tub; safety railings that clamp onto a tub to help you get in and out; and seats that fit across the width of a tub to lessen the strain upon your knees and hips.

Here are a number of self-help devices you can make or improvise to help you with your personal hygiene.

Washing your face

Materials—A 21-inch length of dowel. A two-inch wide spring jaw clamp of the type used for holding papers. Nut and bolt.

Bolt one of the ends of the clamp to the stick. Insert a wash cloth in the clamp and apply to your face. Make sure enough of the wash cloth covers the clamp to prevent the metal from coming in contact with your face.

Combing your hair

Materials—A 21-inch length of dowel. A rat-tailed comb.

Drill hole into one end of stick. Carefully heat tail of comb sufficiently to permit you to bend it until it is practically at right angles to the teeth. Adjust angle to suit you. Force tail into hole you drilled. An all-purpose cement will help hold comb in stick permanently. The hair may now be combed with but a minimum of movement of the arm at either the shoulder or the elbow. If the hand also is involved, it may be necessary to fix the free end of the stick either into a grip made of water-base sculpturing clay or into a carpenter's file handle.

Materials—A rat-tailed comb. A carpenter's file handle.

Insert tail of comb into hole you will find in flat end of file handle. An all-purpose cement will fix comb in place permanently. This device differs from the one described above in that it can be used by persons who still have good motion in their elbows and shoulders but whose hands and fingers are involved.

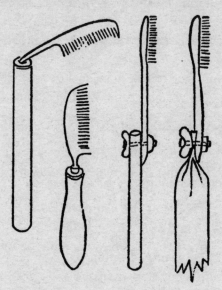

Combs and toothbrushes can be given longer or larger handles. Setting the comb at an angle may help, too.

Brushing your teeth

Materials—A 21-inch length of dowel or an aluminum tube of the same length. An ordinary toothbrush that has a hole in the end of its handle. A bolt with a butterfly thumb-screw nut, the bolt being long enough to go through both the hole in the brush handle and the thickness of the dowel or the aluminum tube.

Drill a hole in the stick, about one inch from the end, that is wide enough to match the hole in the toothbrush handle. If you are using the aluminum tubing, first flatten about two inches of the end before making the hole. Bolt the toothbrush to the stick or to the aluminum tube. The butterfly nut will permit you to adjust the angle of the toothbrush in accordance with your limitations of motion. If your hands are involved too, it may be necessary either to fashion a grip from water-base sculpturing clay or to use the wooden handle of a carpenter's file.

Putting on makeup

Materials—A 21-inch length of doweling. Makeup equipment. A wooden clamp-type clothespin.

Nail one end of clothespin to one end of doweling, so clothespin sets at right angles atop doweling. Clamp various pieces of makeup equipment into place and use.

To help you put on lipstick, there is available commercially a one-piece squared lipstick tube that can be managed with one hand. A slight push of the thumb on a small button flips open the cover of the tube and moves the lipstick into position for use.

Shaving yourself

Materials—A 21-inch length of three-quarter-inch dowel or a length of aluminum tubing of suitable diameter. A lightweight safety razor with a simple, round, slender handle.

In the end of the stick drill a hole of sufficient width and depth to accommodate about two-thirds of the razor handle. Insert same and secure with tape. If you use an aluminum rod make sure it will snugly take the razor handle. If your hand is also involved, it may be necessary to fashion a grip from water-base sculpturing clay or a carpenter's file handle.

Raising your toilet

Materials—Four pieces of two-by-four or two-by-six lumber to make a pedestal as wide and as long as the base of your toilet bowl. This is a job for a plumber.

Most toilets are from 15 to 17 inches in height. The lumber you select will depend upon how high the bowl will have to be to permit you to use it with comfort. You will also need an extra section of connecting drain pipe.

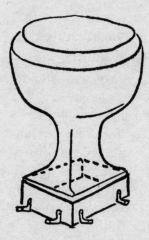

The toilet can be raised to a comfortable height by placing a block under it.

Have a plumber remove the toilet bowl from its floor mountings. Put pedestal in place and secure to floor. Insert and seal section of pipe to connect bowl to drain. Place toilet bowl atop pedestal and secure.

Commercially available are special brackets that will raise the toilet seat from four to six inches without disturbing the bowl.

Taking your bath

Materials—A wooden chair with rubber crutch tips on the legs. A wooden stool also with rubber crutch tips. A rubber suction-type mat. A 12-inch-wide shelving plank, 48 to 50 inches in length. A sheet of waterproof plastic material sufficient to upholster the wooden plank.

You may use either the stool or the chair to sit on in the tub, depending entirely upon the height you need for comfort. Never get into a bathtub unless there is a rubber suction-type mat in it to prevent skidding. The shelving plank will be helpful if you are in a wheel chair. First, however, upholster the plank with the plastic material. To use the plank, you will also need a wooden chair. Roll the wheel chair up against the bathtub, with the flat of one wheel touching the side of the tub. Place plank across tub so that one end overlaps the chair and the other the wheel chair. Slide from wheel chair onto the chair in the tub, lifting your legs over the side of the tub as you get in.

If you are ambulatory, but still with some limited motion, there are a number of devices that will help you bathe with ease and safety. Railings that clamp onto the side of your tub to give you added support as you get in and out, and grab-bars that attach to the walls, are available commercially. If your spine or your back is involved and it is difficult for you to lift your legs over the sides of the tub, lightweight aluminum tent-steps are available. When placed over the side of the tub, they will permit you to step up the outside of the tub and step down on the inside.

Where you can get help for special problems

The self-help devices that can make life easier for you are innumerable. The Self-Help Device Center operated by the Arthritis and Rheumatism Foundation, for example, lists nearly 200 commercially available devices and displays about as many more that have been especially designed for individual problem cases. A feature of the center is the Arthritis Kitchen, designed for women who must be confined to a wheel chair. The kitchen differs from the conventional one. The various work areas are arranged to lessen the need for moving about. Everything is low—low cabinets and low counters. Unique storage spaces beneath the counters and overhead put everything within easy reach with no need for stretching. The toe bases—the recesses of the cabinets at floor level—are high to permit a woman in a wheel chair to get close to the counters.

The service of the Self-Help Device Center is available without cost to arthritics everywhere. If you feel that you may benefit from a self-help device or if you have a particular problem in self-care, you may write the Center at 400 East 34th Street, New York 16, New York. Specialists at the center will discuss and evaluate your problem and either recommend one or more available devices or design special devices.

REMEMBER THESE POINTS
ABOUT SELF-HELP DEVICES

✔ 1. If arthritis has already handicapped you physically, there are certain devices that can help you to live a more normal and independent life.

✔ 2. These devices also help you to conserve energy and protect damaged joints.

✔ 3. A self-help device doesn't have to be elaborate. The ones given in this chapter are simple and easy to make or get.

✔ 4. If you don't find a device for your problem in this chapter you can write for help to the Arthritis and Rheumatism Foundation. (See the last page of the chapter.)

(pages 136-138 combined on this page)

PART **2**

WHAT YOU SHOULD KNOW

ABOUT ARTHRITIS

The person with arthritis who understands what his doctors are trying to do for him, and who has learned how to help his doctors, is the person who will recover. For the arthritic is a necessary teammate, an active partner of his doctor, rather than a passive recipient of treatment.

—from the final report of
a five-year study of arthritis by scientists

~~~ **8**

DON'T FALL FOR
SPECIAL DIETS
OR QUACK CURES

THE ARTHRITIC IS THE MOST EXPLOITED INDIVIDUAL IN THE entire field of health and medicine. He not only spends millions of dollars a year on obvious quack cures but he is even willing to pay a fabulous price for a few pennies worth of fancied-up aspirin, provided the advertising promises an overnight miracle. The more fantastic the claim for a cure, the more eager is the arthritic to buy it and to try it.

When he eventually realizes that he has been taken, he does not seem to complain. He has been fooled so often, that he takes each disappointment in stride. The very next time there is an advertisement for a new cure in the newspapers or on the radio or television, he is again ready to try his luck.

That the arthritic is easy prey for a phony cure and for quacks and charlatans, is not entirely his own fault. The aches and pains that accompany the disease make him desperate in his never-ending search for relief and in his willingness to try anything that promises it.

Being often in agony he doesn't seem to have the patience to consider the long-term arrangement program that is the recognized treatment in the disease. Until a few years ago, there was little that a physician could offer the arthritic other than to send him home and tell him to take it easy. This, over the years, conditioned the arthritic to expect little immediate relief from doctors and certainly no quick cure.

There have been many quack remedies

The arthritic faithfully reads the newspaper ads and tunes in the radio and television, hoping he will discover a cure that doctors have told him does not exist. He listens to relatives and to neighbors and perks up his ears at a "sure cure" handed down by a great aunt or a grandmother from the old country. He carries an old sweet potato in his left hip pocket, provokes a swarm of bees to sting him, has a daily fill of blackstrap molasses and goes to bed with a uranium rock for a pillow. He wears copper bracelets, drinks the juice of one lemon in hot water before breakfast, dusts sulphur into his shoes, and inhales the gasses from a variety of minerals.

Here are still a few more of the many worthless quack remedies that have been used by desperate arthritics in search of a miracle:

A vibrating machine to shake out the arthritis, a daily ration of honey, inner shoe plates made of copper and sprinkled with sulphur, no smoking, smoking three cigars a day, implanting beans under the skin, various herb medicines, a copper wire wound around an inflamed joint, application of boiled poisonous leaves, snake bites, drinking mineral water, conjure bags, health belts, no meat, meat three times a day, mud baths, lemon juice and baking soda cocktail, carrying a horse chestnut in a purse, cream of tartar, ant juice massage, liniments, laxatives, powdered crickets or hornets, lots of vegetable juices, sleeping with the windows tightly closed, leaving all windows open at night, sleeping on the floor and rubbing the painful arthritic limb with a fence slat against which a hog had just scratched itself.

Some quack cures keep coming back

Many cures disappear, never to return again. They are too ridiculous on face value to gain too many adherents. Some though, are revived from time to time.

Two that have completed a cycle and are once again being foisted upon an unsuspecting public are the use of a cocktail made of orange juice and cod liver oil said to be able to lubricate the joints, and a home brew made from alfalfa.

The fact that research has established that arthritis is due to the inflammation of the connective tissue and not to any absence of oils in the joints does not seem to deter the orange-juice—cod-liver-oil cultists. The facts that there are no oils in the human joint, and that the lubricants are made by the joint membrane from simple substances not dependent upon foods or diets, do not seem to make much difference either. Nor does it seem to make any difference to the alfalfa-tea enthusiasts that horses eat alfalfa all their lives and yet suffer from arthritis.

The newest "cures": diets and uranium

Two of the newest quack remedies that have spread across the country are the use of special diets and sitting in a uranium mine. The diet peddler claims that you not only can eat your way into arthritis but that you can also eat your way out again. Thousands of arthritis sufferers have seriously tried the recommended diets and for a time were certain that the long-sought-for miracle had finally been found. They claimed that their aches and pains were gone and that they felt better.

The mine promoter avoided making any claims himself but knew many arthritics who were eager to testify that the days of the vicious disease were at long last numbered. They too no longer had any aches and pains and they too claimed that they were better. That despite the publicity given diet and uranium mines the nation's eleven million arthritis sufferers did not stumble over one another in their mad rush for these two "sure cures" is an indication in itself that the disease had not as yet been conquered. That the thousands who had tried the diets and had visited the mines rarely, if ever, came back for repeated treatments also created doubt about their value.

Why the "cures" seemed to work

Careful medical examination has shown that most arthritis sufferers claiming to have been cured by diet were *self-diagnosed* arthritics. They did not have arthritis; the vague aches and pains they did have were in many instances due to overweight. A loss of a few pounds and they felt better. In those cases where an accurately diagnosed arthritic said he had obtained relief from a special diet, follow-up showed that the improvement was usually temporary. The arthritic, desperately wanting to feel better, began to believe that he did. Mind over matter had brought about temporary improvement. However, in several days or weeks, the pain and distressing symptoms returned. Persons with a true case of arthritis usually gave up trying a diet fad after about four weeks. (The question of diet and nutrition is treated fully a few pages further on.)

About the same can be said for persons who traveled out west for a chance to sit in an abandoned uranium mine. That a vast majority of those who claimed relief from a visit to a radioactive mine did not have rheumatoid arthritis but the vague rheumatic aches and pains almost everyone has, has been indicated by follow-ups of these people. A good many had psychogenic rheumatism, a common ailment brought on by emotional stress and strain in everyday living which usually responds to rest, a change of scene, and a desire to get well. Government atomic scientists checking these mines found that the radiation from the uranium ore wasn't enough to be of any significance. The radon gas in the mines, which the arthritics were encouraged to inhale, was found to be of such low radioactivity that exposure to it could do no good and no harm either.

Four phony-cure peddlers put out of business

A watch-dog committee of the nation's leading arthritis specialists created by the American Rheumatism Association, the parent scientific body of the Arthritis and Rheumatism Foundation, has been quietly working with the Federal government to protect arthritis sufferers from being exploited by quacks and charlatans. That the gullible arthritic is still willing to part with his money in return for some glib promises from some phony medical peddler is evidenced by the fact that during the several months that this book was being written, the committee helped put four bogus-remedy mills out of business.

First, there was the inventor who manufactured and sold pairs of metal plates, one of copper and the other of zinc. Worn inside the arthritic's socks, the copper in the left and the zinc in the right, the plates were supposed to create a beneficial electrical current. No such current ever developed. Then there was the processor who packaged a product of natural vegetation which on its label boldly claimed it was good for rheumatic aches and pains. Analysis proved the vegetation to be nothing more than peat which the promoter had dug up from a peat bog near his home.

Mineral water that was bottled on the West Coast and that sold for $20 a gallon was another miracle cure for every form of arthritis. Upon analysis the water proved to be a sample of the Pacific Ocean with a dash of potassium iodide. Finally, there was the uranium ore packaged in conveniently sized bags to be tucked under a pillow; these bags were shipped to arthritis sufferers over the nation. The uranium turned out to have no greater radioactivity than the average radium-dial wrist watch.

That "cure" was only a coincidence

In any discussion of quack cures, it is difficult to ignore the claims by many properly diagnosed rheumatoid arthritics that despite the fact the treatment they took was non-scientific, they are feeling better. The X ray may still show large areas of joint destruction. Examination may still show the presence of the crippling disease. But when the arthritic who has ached and pained for ever so long says that he is now feeling better, then he must be believed. For no one else but the arthritic can attest to this fact. Why then do some people honestly believe and earnestly insist that though they may have taken a quack remedy, they are feeling better?

The answer lies not in the cocktail made from orange juice and cod liver oil. Nor does the answer lie in the alfalfa tea or the uranium mine. The answer exists in the very nature of the most crippling form of arthritis itself. This chronic arthritis differs from most diseases in that it usually does not run a fast and steady downgrade course until it burns itself out. It is a generally fluctuating disease that has its ups and downs over a number of years. There are times during its course when the arthritis flares up. For days or weeks or even months, the joint soreness and pain may be unbearable. There may be swelling and tenderness. Motion may be practically impossible.

It is at this point that well-meaning friends usually come forward with any number of old and new home remedies. They often are so persuasive that they delay the individual's visit to a physician. Besides, the arthritis sufferer is so desperate for immediate relief from the pain and misery, that he is willing to try anything. What, of course, the friends and the arthritic himself do not know is that just as the disease has flared up, so will it shift to a sudden downward course. Practically overnight the painful symptoms will decrease in severity and the individual will give every indication of getting better. Sometimes the decline of the disease process is so complete that all of the trying symptoms disappear. Now, if an individual with arthritis took orange juice and cod liver oil or alfalfa tea when the disease flared up and was at its worst, it can easily be seen how any of these remedies can be credited with the natural ebbing of the severity of the disease. It would appear that one had something to do with the other.

Some "mistakes" of medical science

Over the years, the medical profession, too, has had its various cures that since have been discarded as being either worthless or impractical. There was a time when it was thought that arthritis was caused by infection. Persons were advised to have all their teeth extracted, their tonsils removed, their sinuses washed out and in the case of men, their prostate gland massaged. For a time, various vaccines were popular and diets and vitamins were tried with great optimism. The dry and warm climate of certain western states was thought to be of value when arthritis sufferers moving there from cold and damp eastern areas wrote back they were feeling much better in their new surroundings. Spas were also advised and, for a time, injections of bee venom were given.

None of these procedures proved to be of any value. There is no recognized arthritis center today that uses vaccines or bee

venom. Extensive research has failed to find any food or vitamin, the presence or lack of which may either cause or cure arthritis. The relief that comes from moving out West proves to
be only temporary and too often is only mental, having been
induced by the change of scene and new-found friends. Besides, studies have shown there is just about as much arthritis
among the native population of these warm dry states as there
is among the natives of cold and wet ones. Spas offer places of
relaxation and the warm mineral pools provide the heat necessary to relieve joint pain. However, the spas or their waters,
apart from their psychological effect, cannot alter the progress of
the disease. The mineral water taken either internally or ex-
ternally has no beneficial effect upon arthritis.

No cure in patent medicines

A day doesn't go by when an arthritic is not subjected to a
high-pressure sales talk regarding a new over-the-counter medicine to relieve the aches and pains of arthritis. If he reads the
printed matter on the package he realizes that these patent
medicines do not offer any cure for the disease. The manufac-
turer promises only to relieve the aches and pains of arthritis
and rheumatism. These medicines that can be bought without
prescription usually are handsomely packaged and high-priced too,
as much as twenty-five cents a tablet. Investigation has shown
that these patent medicines do help relieve body aches and pains
and they do so because *they are basically one-cent aspirin tablets
in fancy dress*. It is the readily available low-priced aspirin within the tablet that provides the relief. Beyond this, these patent
medicines have no curative powers.

Talk to your doctor first

Before you buy any "cure" for arthritis, *think*. Remember
there is no miracle cure for the disease. If you can buy it over

the drugstore counter, then its chief ingredient is probably aspirin or some other analgesic. If it is something that you can get only on prescription, it is for your doctor to decide.

If someone recommends a treatment, discuss it first with your doctor. Should you be ashamed to, a good rule to follow is not to try it. If you do and you are hurt or you delay proper medical care, you will never forgive yourself. The damage that arthritis does cannot be erased or reversed. What is more, the mental letdown and the disappointment you will experience may aggravate your disease even more. It will make you feel far worse than you ever had been before the quack cure was whispered in your ear.

ARTHRITIC DIET vs. THE FACTS

A well-rounded diet is essential to good general health. It is also true that when your health is at its highest possible peak, your resistance to arthritis is at its best.

It is only because of this that nutrition becomes a part of your overall effort to keep your arthritis in check. Otherwise, it would not even be considered in the treatment of the disease.

Arthritis diets may even do harm

There is no special diet for arthritis. You should make no effort to find one or use one. Speaking of special therapeutic diets, Dr. Edward Rosenberg, Chief of the Arthritis Clinic, Michael Reese Hospital, said that they "have generally been based on speculations of rather illogical character. Not one of these diet plans has stood the test of time." *Even trying a diet fad that may appear quite innocent, could prove more harmful than good.* For such diets usually eliminate some particular food or overemphasize some other. The food that has been omitted may be the very one that is essential to your balance of health.

Then again, the food stressed may be one you are allergic to without your knowing it.

People may look alike but beneath it all they may be far from it. Your metabolism—the body chemistry that utilizes your foods—may not be exactly the same as that of your neighbor. Your neighbor may have no trouble eliminating sugar from his diet so as to keep *his* weight down. Yet, sugar may be just what *your* system desperately needs to keep going. Some people have no trouble at all dropping meat entirely from their diet. Others practically collapse without the nutrient values that come from red meats.

Dr. Rosenberg has stated the whole problem of diet in arthritis very well:

"Sufferers include individuals of all age groups, children, mature adults and the aged. Some are overweight and a somewhat larger proportion have lost weight. Some have health problems other than arthritis: allergies, diabetes mellitus, cardiac defects, peptic ulcers, constipation, etc. Each of these additional or complicating defects will dictate its own requirements as to diet and will need proper consideration for planning food intake in these individuals."

So, not only is there no such thing as an arthritic diet but neither is there any single diet that is perfect for everyone. You may eat what you like—provided, of course, that the food agrees with you. Your food may be prepared in just about any manner you please.

It IS important to eat right

Appetite is quite important when it comes to arthritis. A loss of appetite is part of the disease picture. This is the reason, incidentally, that arthritics tend to be a bit underweight. Eating, after all, is a habit. When you don't eat, your stomach shrinks. Soon it takes less and less food to satisfy you. As your weight goes down, so does your resistance.

Doctors will find, at times, that arthritics have developed a complete distaste for food. Forced feedings and extra feedings then become necessary to bring the weight up and with it the body's ability to withstand the presence of the disease. Despite the loss of appetite that accompanies arthritis, you can overcome this problem by making sure that appetizing meals are served you.

Whether the diet you eat is alkaline or acid or whatnot is of little importance. The only requirement is that it be nourishing and that your body be capable of digesting it properly. There are no foods that will find their way any more or any less to your joints than they will to any other part of your body. What is good for *you* is also good for your *joints*. Don't let anyone ever try to tell you any differently. Scientific research has never been able to find any evidence whatsoever that arthritis can be overcome by dietary manipulations.

Generally, arthritis specialists favor a generous but well-balanced intake of food. They favor a diet adequate in protein, carbohydrates, and fat, along with sufficient minerals and vitamins to prevent deficiencies. Also necessary are foods with sufficient residue to minimize constipation. Plenty of meat, eggs, fish, milk and cheese will give you the proteins you will need. Plenty of fresh vegetables will give you the minerals and the vitamins.

If you are overweight, it goes without saying that you should cut down on starches and such things as extra slices of bread, rich desserts, and especially those snacks between meals. If you are underweight, an eggnog or a malted milk between meals or at bedtime may help bring your weight up to what is normal for you. Remember, too much weight can put as much stress and strain upon your body system as too little weight. *So, find out your right weight and stay with it.*

There will also be special dietary problems should you be undergoing treatment with any of the hormones. These drugs have a tendency to accumulate fluids within the body and persons on this medication are usually put on a salt-restricted diet. The hormones also have a way of putting excessive weight on you and so it may be necessary to restrict the intake of calories to keep such gains in check.

Check your diet with your doctor

To obtain a normal intake of all the essential nutrients, you will have to consume several basic foods each day. No one food will provide you with all your dietary requirements. You will also find it much easier to control your weight by eating three proper and complete meals a day. Skipping a meal will only decrease the energy you need so much and so add to your body stress. Besides, when you permit yourself to become hungry, the food that you will eat later in the day to satisfy your appetite will be more than the total intake of three balanced meals.

Dietary requirements vary with the individual. There may be certain nutrients that you will need more than others. There may be some, too, that you do well without. It may therefore be a good idea to discuss the subject of diet with your doctor. Let him check your weight and through various tests establish any nutritional imbalance you may have. Ask him whether any other ailments you may have will interfere with your selection of food. Ask him, too, to check also any food allergies you may have.

Remember, it is the purpose of a properly balanced diet to maintain your ideal weight and your well-being. When your weight is what it should be and when you are at your best nutritionally, the chances are that your general health is at its peak too. When your health is good, you will also find it much easier to overcome your arthritis and stave off any of its threatening damaging effects.

REMEMBER THESE POINTS
ABOUT QUACK CURES AND SPECIAL DIETS

✔ 1. There always have been, and probably always will be, quack cures because some arthritics are desperate and will try anything.

✔ 2. When these "miracle cures" *seem* to work the reasons usually are:
- The person did not have true arthritis in the first place.
- The arthritis cleared up of its own accord at the same time the "cure" was taken.

✔ 3. KEEP THESE POINTS ESPECIALLY IN MIND:
- There is absolutely no miracle cure for arthritis.
- If you buy a patent medicine over the counter, its chief ingredient probably is *aspirin,* no matter how fancy it looks.
- If it's something you can get only on prescription, it is for your doctor to decide.

✔ 4. If you're ashamed to ask your doctor about some "cure," then FORGET IT.

✔ 5. Medical science has proved, over and over again, that there is no such thing as a special therapeutic diet for arthritics. IF A DOCTOR PUTS AN ARTHRITIC ON A DIET IT IS ONLY TO KEEP HIM IN GOOD GENERAL HEALTH, OR TO REGULATE HIS WEIGHT.

~~~ 9

HERE'S THE
WHOLE TRUTH
ABOUT DRUGS

THERE IS BUT ONE "MIRACLE" IN THE TREATMENT OF
arthritis. *It is the skill of the physician in selecting from the
wide range of available drugs and procedures that which is best
for you.*

Except for this, there is no miracle drug and certainly no miracle cure for the disease. Even cortisone and ACTH, the two "wonder drugs" of a few years ago in which so much hope was rested, have proved disappointing and have all but fallen by the wayside. ACTH is hardly being used at all and it is only a matter of time until cortisone, too, will disappear.

Dr. Ralph Boots wrote that the physician "must stress to the patient that no pill or capsule, as yet known, and no combination of oral medications will cure all patients with the disease."

One drug for all arthritics? No!

True, there are a number of drugs now being used in the treatment of arthritis. But their use is limited and in most cases they are prescribed only as a last resort when all other forms of therapy have failed. The basic reason for this is that there is no one drug that will help all arthritics. Only trial and error will let a physician know whether any drug will help a particular person. *Too often, the risk of unwanted side reactions is far greater than the temporary relief that may be obtained with a drug.*

There are two kinds of drugs

Drugs that are being used in the treatment of the severest form of arthritis fall into two categories, the *patent medicines* that are available without prescription and the *more potent ethical drugs* that only your physician can obtain for you. The drugs that are available without prescription are basically *salicylates* of which aspirin is the most common.

Although these drugs ease pain and discomfort, there is no certainty that they have any effect in lessening joint inflammation. Many studies have even shown aspirin is as useful as cortisone in the early stages of the disease.

The more potent drugs, which are available only on prescription, may not only ease joint pain and discomfort but also lessen swelling and suppress or eliminate inflammation. The hope that these drugs might interfere with the disease process itself and perhaps even arrest it, has not been borne out by research. Though used effectively by many physicians, none of these drugs is the final answer nor can any one of them be considered a universally effective treatment, much less a cure.

How does the doctor select the right drug?

Every one of the drugs, even aspirin, used in the treatment of arthritis poses many problems.

A *physician must be able to select a drug he feels will not only help an arthritic, but one that is not likely to hurt him.* He must also be able to devise a pattern of treatment and select a dosage that will give the best possible result with the least possible side effects. The task is not always an easy one no matter how much experience a physician has had with arthritis. Every person with arthritis is an individual problem.

Then, too, each drug will affect different people in different ways. What is more, the effectiveness of a drug varies in long-term and in short-term therapy, as well as in different stages of the disease. The exact mode of action of the various drugs now in use is unknown. The clinical results are based only on practical experience and not on scientific study. *No one knows why these drugs do what they do.* Some of the drugs cause withdrawal problems; that is, the painful and the miserable symptoms of the disease return *with greater impact* when the drug is stopped. Besides, every one of the drugs produces side reactions to some degree, some minor but a good many serious and undesirable.

Arthritis researchers no longer talk about finding a drug that can help everyone. There is too little known about this complex disease even to suggest the development of such a drug. The most that can be said is that the proper treatment consists of the right drug in the right individual at the right time.

Drugs won't CURE Arthritis—yet

In any discussion about drugs, one simple fact cannot be overlooked. Even the ideal drug is able to do no more than ease aches and pains and reduce joint inflammation and swelling.

When cortisone and ACTH were first introduced, it was hoped that these hormones would be able to cure the disease—to clear it up completely. Research has since proved otherwise. The same can be said for a number of other drugs that have since come onto the scene. The chances are that until more is known about the cause of arthritis, and about the exact nature of the disease, there will never be a drug that will be able to cure it.

Warning: leave the decision to your doctor

Before reviewing the various drugs that are now being used, a word of caution is in order.

That a drug has many virtues, does not necessarily mean that it will help *you*. But also, the fact that a drug may produce serious side effects is no indication that it will have the same effect on you.

The decision as to whether you should or should not be given any one drug or another can only be made by your physician, preferably an arthritis specialist. For you to take any of the information you are about to read and use it to insist that your doctor do or do not give you this or that, no matter what he believes is best for you, is certainly foolish and even a bit dangerous. Faith in your doctor is essential in arthritis.

Before we look at each of the drugs, take a glance at the table below. It shows to what extent each one is being used today. It is based on a questionnaire compiled by 284 arthritis specialists who were treating more than 13,000 arthritics.

Aspirin	80%
Gold	28%
Hydrocortisone	21%
Prednisolone	21% (about)
Cortisone	19%

Prednisone	19% (about)
Phenylbutazone	13%
ACTH	3%

THE FACTS ABOUT ASPIRIN

The salicylates, of which aspirin is the most common, are perhaps the only drugs that over the years have been widely and regularly used in the treatment of crippling arthritis. Aspirin in particular has proved to be the most effective and the least dangerous of any drug in relieving *the symptoms* of the disease. Aspirin not only eases aches and pains and joint stiffness, but research indicates that in the early stages of one form of arthritis, the drug lessens the inflammation. But aspirin will suppress the symptoms of the disease only as long as you take it. When you stop taking aspirin the symptoms will return.

Aspirin can help you during the night and in the early morning hours when you are about to get out of bed. It is at these particular times, as you know, that aches and pains and especially joint stiffness are at their worst. A dose of aspirin sometime during the night and another when you awaken will help you over this miserable hurdle.

Unless your doctor has advised you otherwise, you need have no fears about taking aspirin. It is far more important to you and to your recovery that you obtain relief from your arthritis, and avoid any exhaustion that will aggravate the disease, than to avoid taking aspirin. Aspirin will permit you to get more sleep and more rest. As a result, you will be able to eat better, feel better, and more effectively combat the disease. *However, to use aspirin as a means of deadening pain so that you will be able to work all the harder is dangerous.*

Most people can safely take aspirin with hardly any risk at all. Usually two tablets (about 10 grains), taken at intervals through a day, will help keep you comfortable. Often as many as 14 to 16 tablets (70 or 80 grains), and at times even more, may be taken over the period of a day without any harm. You need not fear developing a tolerance for the drug because of prolonged usage. However, because about one out of every 500 or so persons is to some degree sensitive to aspirin, it is advisable that you first check with your doctor before attempting self-medication with any large doses of aspirin.

Many people cannot tolerate the acidity that comes with the use of aspirin. Not only does the drug nauseate them but they quickly develop a feeling of bloating and heartburn. At times they may even throw up. If you are in this group, a little bicarbonate with the aspirin will help. Soda-mint tablets or any other alkali may also be taken with the aspirin. When this is done, dissolve the aspirin and the alkali in a glass of water and take together. Taking aspirin in a glass of milk will also help cut down on the acidity of the drug. There is available commercially a tablet that combines aspirin with an alkali.

Physicians are usually cautious about the use of large doses of aspirin by persons who are allergic to it or who have liver damage or Vitamin K deficiency. *If you have ulcers you should not take ordinary aspirin.* There is available an aspirin with an enteric coating which prevents the tablet from being dissolved and absorbed in the stomach. The coating breaks down in the intestinal tract, where the aspirin is absorbed.

One widespread notion that aspirin can be harmful to the heart is not true at all. Proof of this is that the largest doses of aspirin now in use are prescribed for the treatment of children suffering with rheumatic heart disease.

THE FACTS ABOUT GOLD SALTS

For at least a quarter of a century, injections of gold have been effectively used in the treatment of crippling arthritis. Exactly what gold does once it gets within the body, other than to lodge in the tissues, is not known. It is believed it may have an effect on some of the chemical processes that go on within the body cells. Despite this lack of knowledge, experience has shown that about two out of every three persons given gold undergo a beneficial response. Not only does gold restrict the disease activity, but it also suppresses much of the inflammation.

Over the years, gold has had its ups and downs in popularity. With the widespread disappointment in the hormones, there has been a return to its use. The manner of treatment also has been improved so as to obtain a more prolonged beneficial effect.

Formerly, the drug was given in a series of injections over a period of several weeks or months. Once the disease appeared to be under control, the gold shots were stopped. The beneficial effect would often last for a number of years. When the symptoms recurred, another series of injections was given. Now, instead of completely stopping the shots, the patient is put on continued therapy after the initial series. Booster shots given every two or three weeks maintain a sufficient concentration of gold to keep the disease in check.

Gold is most effective in the early active stages of crippling arthritis. It can only be given by injection, either in a vein or in a muscle. Attempts to give the drug by mouth have proved entirely unsuccessful and there is no gold pill or tablet available.

Whatever good you may obtain from gold injections will not appear dramatically within minutes or hours after treatment. Benefits build up rather slowly over a period of weeks. Sometimes you won't even be aware that you are beginning to feel

better. Often, as much as two months will have to go by before
you will realize that any improvement has taken place. It is
because of this that, too often, gold therapy is discontinued before it has had a chance to prove itself. Many people also become frightened and stop gold treatments when during the first
few injections, they experience an increase in joint soreness and
stiffness. Such a reaction is only temporary.

Gold, like any other drug, is not entirely harmless. It will at
times produce undesirable side effects. In most instances, these
are relatively minor and can be eliminated by merely decreasing
the dosage of the drug. But in about four out of every 100 persons given gold injections, the reactions will be serious enough
to discontinue the treatment. Despite this, there is no reason for
you to fear gold therapy, if that is what your physician feels is
best for you. He wouldn't have recommended gold, had other
more conservative measures been able to help you. Nor would
he have prescribed gold, had he had any reason to believe the
drug would in any way hurt you.

Bear in mind that the benefits you may derive from gold will
greatly outweigh the risk of developing side effects. Besides,
there is now available an antidote for gold toxicity. Known as
BAL, this chemical compound not only can keep undesirable
gold reactions under control, but in an emergency it can be
used to absorb and quickly eliminate the drug from your body.

Summing up the case for gold salts, Dr. Richard H. Freyberg, Director of Arthritis Clinics for the New York Hospital,
said:

"Gold therapy can help only by reducing the inflammation and
checking the progress of the disease and when used it should be
only one portion of a well-planned program of treatment which
should be carefully adjusted to the needs of each individual."

THE FACTS ABOUT HORMONES

Limited though their use may be, the hormones can be quite effective in suppressing the painful and inflammatory symptoms of arthritis. Carefully selected arthritics respond quite well to these highly potent drugs and—with the dosage under control—experience hardly any side reactions. The hormones are usually most effective during the early severe stages of the disease and in arthritics who require but a moderate dosage to obtain beneficial effect. Persons who have had arthritis for one year or less undergo the most striking beneficial results. Those who have had the disease for 10 years or more, experience the least favorable.

From the very outset, when cortisone, the first of the hormones, was introduced, it was known that the beneficial effects of these drugs lasted only as long as they were administered. When the drugs were stopped, the pain, soreness, stiffness, and the many other symptoms of the disease returned. An even more discouraging fact was that the symptoms upon their return were worse than they had been before treatment began. This withdrawal reaction is still one of the major drawbacks of the hormones. However, skilled management and a tapering off of the dosage will often lessen the withdrawal rebound; and there are many cases on record where the improvement was retained long after the drugs were discontinued.

The hormones may yet lead to a drug that will be ideal for the control of arthritic symptoms. Cortisone is a natural body hormone produced by the adrenal glands, which are situated above each kidney. The cortisone that your doctor prescribes, however, is made synthetically. The hope is that by varying and modifying the basic cortisone formula, a new synthetic may result that will have all the beneficial qualities of the original hormone but none of its limitations.

This then would mean a drug that would be highly effective and safe for all arthritics and not just for a select few. Many such variations have been tried and discarded as impractical. Too often when the effectiveness of the original formula was improved the chances of undesirable side reactions were increased too.

Two variations that are now in use are prednisone and prednisolone. Though far from perfect, they are improvements over the original because they are more potent and less toxic.

The way in which the hormones work is not fully understood. Cortisone, when it is administered directly, is known to flood the connective tissue where the disease process is situated. ACTH (its full name is adreno-cortico-trophic hormone) is produced by the pituitary gland at the base of the brain and stimulates the adrenal glands to produce their own hormones. The fact that the hormones bring about quick and dramatic relief, indicates that they produce some chemical change within the diseased connective tissue. Just what that change is, is not known.

When cortisone was first introduced, its dramatic effect led to the belief that arthritics suffered either from diseased adrenal glands or from an insufficient supply of the hormone. This has since been disproved by researchers. The adrenals and the supply of hormones in the arthritic have been found to be essentially of the same quantity and quality as in persons without the disease.

At first, cortisone was given by injection. The initial dose during the first few days was unusually high. When it was certain that joint stiffness and soreness was relieved, the dosage was gradually reduced in a steplike fashion every several days until the symptoms of the disease were suppressed with the least amount of cortisone. This became the maintenance dose for that particular arthritic. It was while the large initial doses were being given that most of the toxic side reactions occurred.

The early trial-and-error experience with cortisone has helped establish a dosage guide that now permits a physician to begin treatment with the minimum amount necessary to produce the desired effect. It is interesting to note that arthritics responding to these drugs now take daily—in tablet form—about one-sixth of the initial daily dose that was prescribed in the early days of cortisone.

That the hormones produce many undesirable side effects cannot be overlooked. For example, about one out of every two persons getting these drugs experiences a serious reaction such as the appearance of peptic ulcers, the retention of salt and water by the body, a weakening of the bones, changes in mood and even mental depression, the aggravation of diabetes, the reactivation of arrested tuberculosis, or the masking of infection. About three out of every four persons experience minor side effects which, while upsetting to the individual, are probably not at all harmful. Among these are rounding of the face, added body fat and weight, abnormal hairiness especially in women, and interference with the menstrual cycle. It is often possible to minimize or eliminate these side effects by simply reducing the dosage of the drugs. However, in many instances, cutting down on the dosage will also reduce their effectiveness.

Arthritis specialists believe that it is neither possible nor wise to attempt to suppress all of the symptoms of arthritis with hormones. Instead, physicians are now satisfied with the amount of improvement and relief that can be achieved with a *moderate and safe dose*. There is also a tendency to use the hormones in conjunction with other drugs, especially with aspirin.

THE FACTS ABOUT PHENYLBUTAZONE

Phenylbutazone is used in the treatment of crippling arthritis more often than is ACTH and almost as much as is cortisone. Yet, there is no agreement among arthritis specialists as to the value of this particular drug. Those who prescribe it think highly of it and point out that though the drug's mode of action is not completely understood, they will continue to use it as long as it is helping their patients and doing so with relative safety. Other physicians, not entirely enthusiastic about the drug, do frankly admit that in a good many cases, "it's a great little pain killer."

Phenylbutazone is a chemical compound and not a hormone. It first made its appearance at about the time cortisone and ACTH were at their height in popularity. As a result, it never enjoyed the publicity and the notoriety that surrounded the two hormones. For that matter, it wasn't until cortisone and ACTH had begun to wane in favor among physicians, that the public began to hear a little about phenylbutazone. During the four- or five-year interval, the drug was kept out of the public eye and was patiently studied in arthritis clinics across the nation. It was found, among other things, that, as with all the other drugs used in the treatment of arthritis, phenylbutazone is best for those who will respond favorably to it. For those who will not or who will suffer unwanted side reactions, the drug is of little or no value.

There is general agreement among physicians on two marked properties of phenylbutazone. First, that it is a highly effective pain killer for inflammatory states, although not for such things as headache. In the early and acute stages of the disease the drug brings about a marked decrease in joint swelling and muscle stiffness. Second, that it has the ability to reduce fever.

Though phenylbutazone is but a chemical compound and in no way related to the hormones, the improvement it brings strangely resembles that resulting from the use of cortisone and ACTH. Within 24 hours after the drug is administered, joint stiffness is reduced. Within a few days, joint tenderness decreases and pain on motion is eliminated. The effect is so striking that many physicians strongly recommend a trial treatment with phenylbutazone before resorting to cortisone and ACTH. The most dramatic effects have been in the most severe cases and unlike cortisone, the drug has been found to be especially useful in long-standing chronic cases.

The side reactions now being experienced with phenylbutazone are not as many or as severe as those reported several years ago. Most of the ill effects were the result of overdosage or the unwise selection of patients. That most of the undesired reactions are now relatively minor, is an indication that as with the hormones the lowest effective dosage is now the rule. Experience has also shown that the elderly arthritic and the one with heart or kidney disease should not be given the drug. Nor should phenylbutazone be given persons with hardening of the arteries and with dietary or nervous disorders.

As with the other drugs used in the treatment of rheumatoid arthritis, once treatment with phenylbutazone is halted, the painful symptoms of the disease will return. However, withdrawal of the drug does not result in any ill effects or flare-ups of the disease. And although persons taking cortisone eventually develop a resistance, persons taking phenylbutazone rarely do.

That drugs are available for the treatment of rheumatoid arthritis is perhaps due to public clamor for such agents. People generally think in terms of drugs when disease strikes. The pressure is now on for a single drug that can be used routinely for everyone when arthritis strikes.

However, the arthritis specialist would rather not use a drug if he can help it. For he knows that no single measure can overcome the effects of the disease. He knows that to be successful, he must create a broad program of treatment made up of many elements and molded exclusively to each particular patient.

REMEMBER THESE POINTS
ABOUT DRUGS

✓ 1. At present—and this goes for the foreseeable future, too—there is no one drug available for the treatment of all arthritics.

✓ 2. The doctor must study all the circumstances of your case and then try to find the drug that *may* help you.

✓ 3. Even the drugs that help you may have undesirable side effects, so the doctor has to think about that, too.

✓ 4. NO DRUG WILL CURE ARTHRITIS. It *may* ease pain, reduce swelling, and cool inflammation.

✓ 5. Drugs are complicated things. You can ask your doctor about them, but LEAVE THE DECISION UP TO HIM.

(pages 168-170 combined on this page)

≈ 10

THE KIND OF ARTHRITIS CALLED RHEUMATOID

To SAY THAT YOU HAVE ARTHRITIS, IS MERELY TO SAY THAT your joints are inflamed and that they hurt. Like a headache, arthritis may be brought on by any number of varied diseases and physical conditions.

As the word stands alone, *arthritis* is not a disease at all but the name for a group of joint symptoms: aches, pains, swelling, inflammation, stiffness, and at times, crippling. To the doctor it is meaningless to use the word by itself. Yes, you may have arthritis. But what kind do you have?

There are as many as fifty different important forms of arthritis and about one hundred variations of these. But only two of the forms together make up more than 70% of all rheumatic complaints. They are *rheumatoid* arthritis and *osteo*-arthritis. In this chapter we will discuss the rheumatoid kind.

RHEUMATOID ARTHRITIS AND ITS CAUSES

Rheumatoid arthritis is the more serious of the two. It is a progressive disease of the entire body system. Although it is more evident around the moveable joints, it may occur almost anywhere in the body.

Rheumatoid arthritis strikes young and old alike. Children as young as six months of age have been known to have the disease. Usually it starts between the ages of 20 and 45 with most cases occurring between 35 and 40. It affects three times as many women as men. However, when it concentrates itself in the spine, it strikes 10 times as many men as it does women.

Rheumatoid arthritis will smolder quietly in the body, often for years, before it mushrooms up with all its miserable and painful symptoms. The various signs may come on suddenly or —as it more often happens—build up gradually.

Rheumatoid arthritis shows a definite pattern. In three out of four cases, the disease maintains a steady, at times fluctuating, downward course. The disease has a very definite beginning, though it is not often or easily recognized, and it has an end, too, when the process burns itself out, leaving as mysteriously and as quietly as it came.

Every attack of rheumatoid arthritis is not necessarily a bad one and neither does the disease always get worse.

Dr. Charles Ragan, of Columbia Presbyterian Hospital, has said that "the progress of the disease may be interrupted temporarily or permanently at any stage so that no patient with rheumatoid arthritis should be considered as beyond aid."

But should an attack be unduly vicious, it may leave deformities of the joints. No joint in the body is immune to this irreparable destruction. The tiniest joints in the spine are at times impaired. The knees are very often affected. The jaw, the only joint in the head, has also been known to be involved. It is the joints of the fingers, however, that are usually stricken most often and most severely.

WHAT SCIENCE THINKS ABOUT
THE CAUSES OF RHEUMATOID ARTHRITIS

Rheumatoid arthritis doesn't just happen. Something has to cause it. And why does it strike some individuals and not others?

There are almost as many theories about what causes rheumatoid arthritis as there are forms of the disease. Though there is some basis for each theory, none has given the whole answer. No matter how many arthritics may be found to support a particular theory, more can be found who are exceptions.

Can it be infection?

Many facts tend to support the theory of *infection*. Rheumatoid arthritis will at times begin after an attack of tonsillitis, a severe cold, or an infection of the gall bladder. Upon removal of the tonsils or the gall bladder or upon the clearing up of the cold, the joint pain and swelling will often disappear.

Under certain conditions, an infection will also influence an already existing case of rheumatoid arthritis. For example, a person with the disease will feel worse when he develops an infected tooth. The localized infection, in this case, seems to tax the body's defenses, thus aggravating the arthritis. Once the tooth is removed and the infection clears up, the aches and pains will *diminish*. But the disease is still there, very much alive and active.

There is other apparent support for the theory of infection. For example, rheumatoid arthritis and infection have much in common. Both produce swelling, redness, tenderness, and heat. Both cause pain and at times a slight fever with perhaps even an increase in the heart beat. What is more, many of the laboratory tests used to detect a serious infection will also give a positive reaction in rheumatoid arthritis.

In the past few years, interest in infection has been revived. One research group has been pursuing the theory that the disease may be caused by a virus. They have even been treating several thousand arthritics with a powerful antibiotic drug. Nothing conclusive has appeared on this yet.

Can it be nutrition?

One of the most popular theories, one that from time to time has caught the interest of the general public, is that rheumatoid arthritis is caused by some deficiency in diet or in vitamins.

The theory that people are what they eat, the implication that illness is related to diet and nutrition, is not entirely new. Any individual who will propose a two-day or a five-day or a thirty-day diet to cure arthritis will, for a little while, find an eager and receptive audience.

It is hoped that the information in Chapter 8 will put an end to the theory that arthritis is caused by a nutritional lack.

Another fad, that of not drinking water with meals, also has no basis in scientific truth. There is no evidence that drinking water has any affect whatever upon arthritis. Nor is there a relationship of any kind between constipation and arthritis.

The use of orange juice and the Vitamin C it contains as a treatment for rheumatoid arthritis is also scientifically incorrect. Vitamin C, contrary to the claims of orange-juice faddists, plays absolutely no part in lubricating the joints, though it is used by the adrenal glands. The scientific truth is that cortisone and hydrocortisone, the two anti-rheumatic hormones produced by the adrenal gland, are made from very simple substances and not from any vitamins or other foods.

Can it be glandular?

That rheumatoid arthritis is caused by a *glandular* disturbance is one of the few theories that for a time appeared to have been scientifically proved. Several years ago, research scientists enthusiastically hailed the discovery of cortisone, a natural body hormone, as the long-awaited cure. For quite a while, observations had pointed to just such a hormone as the possible final solution to the age-old problem of rheumatoid arthritis. You have seen in the last chapter that cortisone, unfortunately, was not the answer.

But when cortisone first came on the scene, many physicians who had felt that rheumatoid arthritis was due to a glandular deficiency, were now certain they had been correct.

Recent research, however, has failed to support the gland theory. The gland in persons with the disease is just as active as in those without any arthritis. What is more, persons with Addison's disease, in which the adrenal glands are so badly damaged they are practically useless, do not get rheumatoid arthritis.

Still, many researchers hold to the theory. They point out that the disease seems to show preference for women, and that in women it will strike most often between the ages of 20 and 35, the child-bearing years when the demands upon the body's glands are greatest. The disease also is known to flare up during a woman's monthly periods and to occur at menopause, a time of life when changes in body hormones put an end to menstrual periods.

Then too, there is the ever-present observation that women with rheumatoid arthritis who become pregnant, experience immediate and gratifying relief from the effects of the disease. Not only does the arthritis lessen in severity but in most cases the distressing symptoms will disappear entirely until after the birth of the baby. (It was this phenomenon that led to the discovery of cortisone.)

But against all that is the fact that men get the disease, too.

Efforts to treat rheumatoid arthritis with sex hormones have proved unsuccessful. Even attempts to inject blood taken from pregnant women and to implant tissue taken from the after-birth, in the hope of transmitting anti-rheumatic hormonal activity, have also failed. Whatever good results were obtained with these procedures proved to be only temporary responses due more to the mental desire of the arthritic to get well, than to any real curative powers in the hormone.

Can it be emotional?

One of the oldest theories is that the disease will start after a strong emotional upheaval, after some highly disturbing experience. From a close look at the case histories of persons with the disease, it would appear that this could very well be so.

In a good many instances, especially among women, rheumatoid arthritis will actually strike for the first time immediately after some highly distressing personal incident. What is more, once the disease has made its presence felt—regardless of what triggered the attack—worry and emotional tension will aggravate the painful and distressing symptoms.

A check of the case histories of thousands of women patients at arthritis clinics across the nation, showed that *mental stress* was most certainly a part of the life pattern of a good many of them. In a surprisingly large number of instances, marital difficulties were the causes of the emotional disturbances that had actually preceded the onset of the disease. Threats to personal or family security and family financial problems figured highly as the causes for the emotional upsets.

Other emotional experiences that were found to have preceded the initial attack of rheumatoid arthritis were: sudden death in the family, worry over the severe illness of a loved one, the loss of employment, working at a job that was most disliked, and working for an unpleasant employer or with difficult co-workers. In each of these varied instances, either the sudden blow or the prolonged mental strain had been followed—often immediately—by the first sensations of stiffness in the hands or in the knees, the first symptoms that rheumatoid arthritis had struck.

One unusual experience concerned a young man in his mid-twenties. He was a clerk in a small neighborhood grocery. He liked his job and he was determined to learn all he could about the business so that one day he would be able to open a grocery of his own. His employer was a reasonable fellow and he had no cause for complaint. The only unpleasantness was the role he often was called upon to play, as peacemaker between his employer and the employer's wife. The two constantly argued and bickered over personal as well as business and financial matters.

One day, during a rather heated quarrel, the couple came to blows. Shouting, "I'll show you what I can do," the grocery store owner suddenly snatched up a large knife from the counter and lunged at his wife. He made no more than one broad sweep with the heavy blade. His wife collapsed.

The young clerk who witnessed the incident fainted. He was revived, given sedatives to calm him down, and sent home with orders to rest. Try as he would to rest, the nervous tension that had welled up within him would not be released. He told doctors later that he felt like a bundle of jittery nerves all tied up in one complicated knot.

The next morning on awakening, the grocery clerk could barely get out of bed. His entire body ached and pained. Every joint was sore and stiff and several were even inflamed. There was no doubt about the symptoms nor about what the examination and subsequent tests indicated. The shock had brought on a sudden and severe case of rheumatoid arthritis.

Despite all the evidence that has been gathered, the theory that rheumatoid arthritis is an emotional disease wants much before it can be accepted. The simple fact is that *everyone* at some time or other has experienced a highly emotional and upsetting situation. Everyone has gone through at least one period of serious illness involving a loved one, or has lost a dear one or has a tyrant for a boss. Yet, not everyone suffers an arthritis attack. What is more, not every case of rheumatoid arthritis has been known to follow or even to be involved with any shocking or highly emotional experience.

Can it be climate?

Men of medicine and their patients have, for centuries, condemned the vagaries of climate as the cause of rheumatic complaints.

Cold, dampness, and chilling have long been suspected of a connection with rheumatoid arthritis. Persons with the disease tend to be acutely sensitive to changes in the weather, feeling better on hot, dry days or on cold, dry days and worse when it is hot and humid or cold and damp. Recent studies even indicate that the incidence of the disease begins to rise sharply in November when the winter season starts. Persons who already have the disease seem to feel worse during April when the rainy season is at its height.

There is the generally accepted fact that rheumatoid arthritis is found primarily in the temperate climates and is quite rare in the hot, dry tropics and in the cold, dry arctic regions. Spas in cold and damp Northern Europe, for example, have large numbers of arthritic guests, while those located in warm and dry Southern Europe have very few. In this country, too, there is said to be a higher incidence of the disease along the storm-ridden North Atlantic coastline.

Here is a very interesting fact in favor of the climate theory. The remains of dinosaurs that had inhabited the Gobi Desert in Mongolia when the area was hot and dry, show no signs of arthritis. However, the bones of the mammoth beasts that had lived in the area when the desert's climate had changed to include a cold season, with its damp weather, show very definite signs of the disease.

Yet there is still doubt. Dr. W. Paul Holbrook, Director of Research at the Southwestern Clinic and Research Institute, has written:

"Cold, dampness and chilling have been condemned for centuries by patients and physicians as predisposing to the onset or aggravating rheumatic diseases. However, there are very few precise data to support such a contention."

For the truth is there is as much arthritis among the native population of some of this country's hot and dry southwestern states as among the cold and damp northeastern ones. Rheumatoid arthritis may be just as severe and as crippling in the center of the Arizona desert as it may be in the damp lowlands of Brooklyn, New York.

In Europe, too, as much rheumatic disease has been found high in the dry rocky hills of Sweden as in Holland which is mostly damp and below sea level.

It is quite doubtful that weather or climate as such has any effect on the incidence of rheumatoid arthritis. About all that can be said with certainty is: when the disease already is present, climate or changes in weather may aggravate the complaint in some people.

This may be the answer

In reading through the above theories, it may have occurred to you that they all have something in common. Each one represents some form of *stress*, some challenge to the body's natural processes. Each represents some form of pressure upon a person's internal well-being.

Dr. Joseph L. Hollander, of the University of Pennsylvania, has observed "it is becoming increasingly apparent that prolonged or abnormal stresses are intimately associated with the onset of the rheumatic diseases."

The theory of stress, as developed by Dr. Hans Selye of Canada, points out that when a person enjoys good health, it is because of a reasonable balance among all of his many body processes. There is a definite harmonious relationship, it states, between respiration, digestion, the activity of the blood, the production of hormones, the behavior of certain chemical systems, and all the other body processes that make life possible. Should stress disturb any single process, not only will the particular functions dependent upon it be affected, but the entire natural balance among all of the body processes will be in danger.

Should the disturbance go no further than a single body process, the result may be no more than a simple disease: a bad cold, indigestion, or perhaps even the flu. However, should the balance among many or most of the body processes be severely disturbed, the result may be a more complicated chronic disease, such as rheumatoid arthritis. (It is interesting to note that temporary joint aches and pains often accompany many ailments.)

But *stress* still isn't the whole story.

That the various contributing causes will trigger the start of the disease *in some persons and not in others*, indicates the importance of still another element, *the individual*. It is becoming more and more apparent that it is the stuff a person is made of that will determine whether rheumatoid arthritis will or will not strike. There is growing evidence that persons who do suffer an arthritic breakdown, do so *because they have inherited a susceptibility to the disease*.

Russell L. Cecil, Medical Director of the Arthritis and Rheumatism Foundation, when asked by patients whether they have done anything to help bring on the disease, always answers: "You made a mistake in selecting your ancestors."

It is only quite recently that researchers have begun to appreciate the importance of heredity in rheumatoid arthritis. Family studies of persons with the disease have turned up many relatives who also have some form of the disease, *far more than chance alone could provide*. Almost every arthritic seems to have cousins, aunts, uncles, and grandparents who suffer from one form of arthritis or another. *Studies have shown that rheumatoid arthritis occurs six times more often among relatives of persons with the disease than among families in the general population.*

That it isn't heredity alone, but the combination of a susceptible individual under the pressure of a contributing factor, that will bring about an attack of rheumatoid arthritis, was demonstrated dramatically by one extensive controlled study. Researchers selected 532 persons with the disease and compared them with 532 persons without the disease.

Three things were learned from the study. First, that both groups had experienced about the same stresses and strains in life. Second, that in the arthritic group, these same pressures were the contributing causes. Third, that *the only significant difference between the two groups was that the arthritics had a far higher proportion of relatives who were also arthritics*. It was apparent then that the single factor that had made the difference between whether arthritis did or did not strike was *heredity*.

The story of the part heredity plays in arthritis is also the story of a young woman who, from her farm home in North Carolina, fought back against the disease that had made her a wheel-chair invalid.

At thirteen Evelyn Hendricks was stricken with rheumatoid arthritis. Moving swiftly in her case, within three years the disease had reduced her to helplessness. When she had recovered from the shock of being struck down in the prime of life, she began her counterattack—and not just at the disease in her own body. She went after the mystery of arthritis itself.

She set out to learn everything she could about the disease. She attended medical lectures, read medical books and journals with the aid of a dictionary. Somehow, she began to feel that in her own life was concealed the answer to the disease that had puzzled physicians for ages.

Evelyn Hendricks had never finished high school. But she had natural intelligence and something that made all the difference: *desire*.

She wrote to arthritis specialists asking about their experience. She contacted authors of textbooks and medical papers, asking about things she didn't understand. She offered her own body to research groups for experiment.

In every letter she wrote, Evelyn Hendricks observed that a review of her family had shown a surprising number of relatives stricken with arthritis. "Does this mean anything?" she would ask.

The nation's most eminent arthritis specialists took time out to reply to her questions and encourage her. Some offered advice, assistance, and the use of their names. Others opened their research files and arranged for her to get medical data from hospital centers.

The medical staff at Duke University volunteered to conduct detailed physical examinations of all arthritis suspects she listed in her studies.

She interviewed every living relative she could find; delved into family Bibles, legal documents, and old records of country doctors to learn about relatives long gone.

She found 20 cases of crippling arthritis few had suspected even existed. She found that one of her brothers had spondylitis, crippling arthritis of the spine. She found rheumatic diseases among many young members of the family.

She recorded comments by her grandmother and a great-aunt and found evidence that many of her kinfolk long had believed "rheumatism runs in families."

Before she finished she had studied 2,000 members of her family, living and dead. She had presented the strongest possible evidence that arthritis is hereditary.

Today, Evelyn Hendricks continues her studies of arthritis, a respected researcher, with the assistance of two doctors and a grant from the Federal government.

Because this woman *didn't give in* when arthritis wracked her body and crippled her, we are closer than ever to conquering the disease for good.

Inherited constitutional weakness is such an integral part of the human being that it cannot be corrected. But the pressures that strain the body's inherited traits can be controlled. It is possible with common sense and proper care to ease the many stress factors that challenge the various body processes.

REMEMBER THESE POINTS
ABOUT THE KIND OF ARTHRITIS
CALLED RHEUMATOID

✔ 1. Rheumatoid arthritis can appear suddenly after smoldering undiscovered for years, or it can come on gradually.

✔ 2. IF YOU HAVE A STRONG ENOUGH DESIRE TO GET WELL, AND PERSEVERE IN TREATMENT, RHEUMATOID ARTHRITIS CAN BE INTERRUPTED TEMPORARILY OR PERMANENTLY AT ANY STAGE.

✔ 3. There are many theories about the causes of rheumatoid arthritis, but they all seem to boil down to two things: *stress and heredity.*

✔ 4. You can't do anything about your inherited bodily traits, but you *can* avoid many of the stresses in life.

THE KIND OF
ARTHRITIS
CALLED OSTEO

IF IT IS *osteo*-ARTHRITIS THAT YOU HAVE, YOUR OUTLOOK for a normal life, free of pain and certainly free of crippling, is good. Despite the fact that you have a chronic, and in a sense, incurable ailment, you will have little trouble learning how to live with it.

At its worst, osteo-arthritis will prove to be no more than a painful nuisance that with the proper attitude and the mildest of drugs will be most bearable. It may curtail your activity somewhat, but it will certainly not stop you altogether.

Of all the forms of arthritis, this is by far the most common. To say that almost everyone has the ailment isn't too far from the truth. It has been estimated that as many as 95% of all persons past the age of 40 have osteo-arthritis to some degree. It has also been said that if you live long enough you will most certainly come down with the ailment. Fortunately, only about one out of every ten persons develops severe symptoms.

Osteo *is really a misleading name*

Osteo-arthritis at one time was called *menopausal* arthritis, because it so often occurs in women during their change of life. Another name for it was *hypertrophic* arthritis, because quite often the ends of the bones in involved joints became enlarged. The more common term, *osteo*-arthritis, which means an inflammation of a joint and its bone, is not only incorrect medically, but is also misleading. Too often in the minds of the public it is confused with the more serious rheumatoid arthritis, thus leading to unnecessary fears.

By far the most accurate name for the ailment is *degenerative joint disease*. For osteo-arthritis is really a deterioration of the working parts of the joint.

One noted arthritis specialist points out that osteo-arthritis is to the joints what hardening of the arteries is to the blood vessels. In hardening of the arteries, the arteries lose their elasticity. They become thick, undergo some inflammation, and even show signs of degeneration. In osteo-arthritis, the joint, too, loses its flexibility. The bone begins to harden and break down, the cartilage starts to deteriorate and the fine membrane lining begins to thicken. There may also be inflammation of the supporting structure of the joint.

There are two varieties of osteo-arthritis, one *local* and the other *general*. The local occurs in a single joint and has a specific cause such as an injury, a serious infection, or a deformity at birth. The generalized form may affect several joints at the same time; and though aging and wear and tear are definite contributing factors, it may also occur for no apparent reason at all.

Whether it is local or general, the deterioration that takes place in the joints is the same. Whether it is one joint or more that have been stricken, the pain, stiffness, and the loss of motion are the same too.

Part of the cause may be aging

Osteo-arthritis is in some way related to aging. The ailment is rarely seen in persons under 40. It occurs in younger individuals only when it is caused by injury or by artificial menopause. Wear and tear, resulting from overuse of the joint, are involved, too.

But there may be other factors that are as yet unknown. For example, in many cases wear and tear do not seem to play a role at all. Joints that are hardly used, such as the first joints of the fingers, are quite often affected. Affliction of this sort is mainly a disease of middle-aged women, and it starts around the age of 40. It strikes ten women for every man and seems to be passed on from mother to daughter. Some persons also appear to be more susceptible to joint breakdown than others.

The role of heredity is highly suspected, since the disease tends to travel in families.

Persons who get osteo-arthritis usually are stocky and broad-shouldered. Among men, they invariably are the robust and muscular individuals. Among women, they are not only the hefty and chunky types, but also women who are at menopause.

In the overweight woman, the knees and the back will be affected; and the greater the weight, the greater the joint damage.

The joints that are most affected by osteo-arthritis are not only those that over a period of time have been subjected to the stress and strain of weight-bearing, but those that over the years have also undergone wear and tear brought on by occupational (or other) overuse.

Day laborers, for example, are quite prone to the ailment, usually developing it in the spine and in the knees. Occupations that call for poor posture are often at fault. Poor posture will strain muscles and thus weaken joints, bringing on irritation and osteo-arthritis.

The unequal distribution of weight in a joint brought on by some deformity will help cause osteo-arthritis too. For example, persons who are bow-legged or knock-kneed develop the ailment in their knees. Those with spinal curvatures and deep swaybacks will develop the ailment at the bases of their spines. A joint that has been the site of a chronic infection, such as tuberculosis, may also develop osteo-arthritis.

Early signs of osteo

The early symptoms of osteo-arthritis are basically the same as those experienced throughout the presence of the disease. They are primarily pain and stiffness that occur upon motion and the use of the affected joint. A clue that the disease threatens is a joint pain that increases and worsens with prolonged activity but is relieved by rest. Another warning sign is a feeling of stiffness upon getting up from a seated position. The discomfort, though, is of short duration and the aches quickly disappear once you start moving about. Weakness, anemia, and loss of weight, so frequently seen in rheumatoid arthritis, do not occur at all.

Most commonly involved are the joints of the hips, knees, and the lower spine. The most obvious signs of osteo-arthritis develop in the end joints of the fingers where hard bony knots or protrusions appear. These bony enlargements or nodules, though they are usually painless, often will arouse the fear that rheumatoid arthritis has struck and that crippling has already begun. Such fear is unfounded, for rheumatoid arthritis rarely affects the end joints of the fingers.

Osteo-arthritis can strike the spine

In osteo-arthritis of the spine, the pain will often confine it-self to the base of the spine, though at times it will radiate around the small of the back. The pain will be made worse by a vigorous cough or a sneeze. Should the uppermost sections of the spine become involved, there may be headache, earache, sore throat, and neuritis pains in the arms and fingers with some pain and stiffness about the neck and shoulders.

And it can attack the hips

In osteo-arthritis of the hips, the earliest symptom is a puz-zling and mysterious pain that slowly invades the area and grad-ually radiates down into the groin and inside the thigh. Pain and discomfort increase with motion. Stiffness often follows and movement may be sufficiently restricted so that the person de-velops a characteristic limp or shuffle. The ailment seems to fa-vor men, with laborers and former athletes among its choice vic-tims. Though both hips may be stricken, the disease more often affects only one.

When the destructive overuse of a joint is due to occupation, only the single joint seems to be involved. On the other hand, when the cause is not that specific, any number of weight-bear-ing joints may be affected. In men, the lower spine and the hips are stricken most often. In women, the fingers, knees, and upper spine are the most common sites.

Here's a picture of osteo-arthritis at work

Were it possible to watch the gradual breakdown of a joint stricken with osteo-arthritis, you would also be witnessing a joint undergoing the normal process of aging. For, when observed from within, the changes that take place during osteo-arthritis are no different from those that occur as you grow older nor-

mally. The only difference is that the process is somewhat ac-
celerated. It is as if the joint were aging faster than the body
around it.

There was but once in your lifetime that the joints of your
body were normal in every respect. That was in childhood before you were ten years old. During those early years the most
powerful microscope would have had trouble revealing the tiniest flaw anywhere in any joint. The cartilage was a translucent
bluish-white that actually glistened with life. It was as smooth as
it possibly could be. The synovial membrane, lying innocently
nearby, had that fresh, unwrinkled, pinkish look reserved only
for the newborn.

As you got into your teens, a change took place. At certain
points in the joint structure, the synovial membrane began to
thicken. Here and there it became densely calcified. Its surface
began to take on a roughened appearance. A close look with a
microscope would have revealed tiny tufts marring the once perfect face of the membrane.

It wasn't until you were about 21 that the first real change,
the first true abnormality, appeared in your joints. The cartilage
was no longer the translucent bluish-white of your earlier years.
It had become opaque and had turned yellowish. Its elasticity,
too, was gone. Its once smooth and glistening surface was now
slightly uneven and rough. Here and there shallow ridges were
beginning to spread in all directions.

Looking back, these changes in the cartilage were the very first
signs of aging. As you grew older, the aging process continued to
be etched in this soft bony structure. With age, the roughness
in the cartilage increased. The ridges in it became more pro-
nounced. The surface started to shred and the once polished and
smooth cartilage now took on a velvety appearance. The greatest
changes took place in the weight-bearing portions of the joint.

By the time you reach 60, chances are the cartilage begins to deteriorate in earnest. Like parched fallow land in a drought, it becomes pockmarked with pits, crevices, and deep erosions. Here and there it begins to fray as if something has been nibbling away at it. Coarse and brittle and practically lifeless, it will slowly begin to thin and disintegrate.

This then is normal aging. It is a constant and an apparently predetermined pattern, a way of life that begins at a specific point and follows a very definite course to an ultimate conclusion. This, too, is osteo-arthritis; but osteo, because of its hurried pace in certain weight-bearing joints, becomes a disease instead of a natural body process.

The weight of your body is partly to blame

There is as yet no explanation of why natural aging will suddenly step up its tempo to become osteo-arthritis. Because the hips, the knees, and the spine are the sites of the earliest symptoms of the disease, it is believed the pressures of weight-bearing must be involved. A close examination of any of these joints will show that even normally the greatest wear is at the points of greatest weight. However, the exact mechanism by which joint activity contributes to the development of osteo-arthritis is not really known.

Moderation is the keynote in treatment

In the following sentences, Dr. Joseph Hollander, of the University of Pennsylvania, has struck the keynote for treatment of osteo-arthritis:

"Since wear and tear and obesity are known factors in osteo-arthritis, a doctrine of temperance in all things should be preached. By temperance is meant moderation, not the currently used corruption of the term to denote total abstinence. This covers moderation in the activity of the patient, frequent light activity rather than prolonged or severe exertion, and certainly not continuous inactivity either. Moderation in dietary habits is essential. Television has had a double bad effect on osteo-arthritis—the patient often sits for long periods without moving and also eats large quantities of snack foods. Poor sitting posture likewise helps aggravate spinal osteo-arthritis symptoms, so we usually demand moderation of television viewing."

Some false ideas about osteo-arthritis

As with rheumatoid arthritis, many erroneous ideas have sprung up about osteo-arthritis. Here are the answers to several of the more common untruths about the disease.

Osteo-arthritis is not due to bacteria or to poisons in the blood, and it has nothing to do with the amount of acid in the body. The disease is not brought on by deficiencies in diet nor by the lack or presence of any food or vitamin. Snaps, cracks, or creaks in the joints are not an indication that osteo-arthritis is developing and there is no evidence that abnormalities of any glands are to blame. If you have the ailment, cold and dampness may aggravate your aches and pains, but they will not cause the disease.

That osteo-arthritis will not make a helpless cripple out of you has already been pointed out. To that might be added that, although persons with rheumatoid arthritis may after a while develop the osteo kind too, osteo-arthritis will not lead to the development of the more serious rheumatoid kind.

REMEMBER THESE POINTS
ABOUT THE KIND OF ARTHRITIS CALLED OSTEO

✔ 1. Osteo-arthritis isn't as serious as the rheumatoid kind. It may slow you down but it will never stop you altogether.

✔ 2. A more accurate name—one that medical science uses —is *degenerative joint disease*. That name really describes it: a breaking down or wearing out of the working parts of the joints.

✔ 3. Osteo-arthritis is almost certainly related to aging, but science still doesn't know exactly how.

✔ 4. It is known, too, that *overweight* is part of the cause, since your joints bear the constant pressure of your weight.

✔ 5. Since wear and tear and overweight are factors in osteo-arthritis you should practice *moderation* in everything you do. In other words: TAKE IT EASY!

∿ 12

SOME OTHER KINDS OF ARTHRITIS

SEVERAL OTHER DISEASES, DIFFERENT IN CAUSE, NATURE, and treatment from rheumatoid and osteo, cause arthritis-like pain and disability and are listed as arthritic diseases.

Although this book was written for the great mass of sufferers from rheumatoid and osteo, we will say a word about those other, less common forms.

GOUTY ARTHRITIS

Though gout is associated with arthritis, it is a disease in its own right. The association is simply that gout will often cause arthritic damage to the joints. But there are numerous other complications. For example, the disease is known to damage the kidneys badly. When it settles in the joints and causes swelling, pain, and at times crippling, it is referred to as *gouty arthritis*.

Though usually depicted as striking the foot, especially the big toe, the arthritic symptoms may settle most anywhere.

Gout is inherited

The basic cause of gout is not known, but the process is fairly well understood. It is a generalized disease that affects the entire body. It is a result of an inherited defect in the body metabolism, the chemical processes that turn food into energy. This defect prevents the consumption of *purines*, a group of chemical compounds found in certain foods. The purines, which are the base substance of *uric acid*, accumulate in the system resulting in an excess of acid in the blood.

As the blood stream becomes saturated with uric acid, this waste product of metabolism spills over and deposits itself almost anywhere in the body. It more often, though, finds its way into the joints, where it lodges and crystallizes. The uric acid crystals that result irritate the highly sensitive joint mechanism. Scarring and inflammation take place and arthritis follows.

It is as if sand were poured into the precision-built smoothly moving parts of the engine. The scarring and inflammation, incidentally, may affect different tissues of the body in different ways. In the blood vessels it produces hardening of the arteries. In the kidney it lessens efficiency and may even lead to the formation of kidney stones.

Though the defect that leads to gout is present at birth, the disease, as a rule, does not occur until later in life. Gout favors men over women, 19 to 1, and usually affects men between the ages of 30 and 50. It is the most common cause of arthritis in men past the age of 40. Gout rarely affects women before the menopause; and when it does strike, it is far less severe than in men. Gout is not a disease of rich people nor does it favor any particular racial group as it was once believed. The disease strikes the wealthy and the poor alike.

Though certain foods high in purine content are best avoided, the disease is not exclusive with persons who indulge in rich foods and in alcoholic beverages. For the purines that accumulate in the body, although largely derived from the foods you eat, are also the result of normal wear and tear and the replacement of cells within your body. Old and used cells are burned up by the body and a quantity of purine results.

Treatment of gouty arthritis is specialized

The treatment of gout begins with several general measures to ease the effects of the painful disease. During an acute attack you should make every effort to rest the affected joints. It may even be necessary to rest in bed. If only an elbow or a hand is involved, an arm sling may provide sufficient rest. If your foot is involved, you should replace your shoe with a bedroom slipper.

The use of heat, wet packs, or cold compresses is *not* advisable in easing the painful symptoms of gout. Your diet should be light and you should drink about eight glasses of water a day to provide a vehicle for the release of uric acid through the kidneys. Regardless of the severity of the disease, it is most desirable that you have an abundant intake of water so as to prevent the formation of kidney stones. Plain drinking water is best. Milk, soft drinks, and other calorie-loaded fluids will only help increase your weight and thereby aggravate the disease.

There was a time when gout sufferers were maintained on a rather strict diet stripped of all purines and proteins. However, with the realization that the disease is due to an inherited defect, and that it is not only diet that may be involved, restrictions on the use of certain foods have been eased greatly. *It was also found that a rigid control of the formation of uric acid through diet was impossible simply because a person could not live on a diet that excluded all the substances that can be converted to uric acid.*

However, a certain few foods, which are known to cause a marked increase in uric acid production, may well be avoided. These foods may be left out of your diet without any fear of developing dietary deficiencies. They are: anchovies, brains, kidney, liver, meat extracts, sardines, and sweetbreads.

A number of drugs have proved useful in the treatment of gout. Three of these, *phenylbutazone, aspirin,* and *benamid,* help the body excrete the accumulated uric acid from the blood.

The fourth, *colchicine,* had been successfully used for many years, though the manner in which it is able to ease the effects of the disease is not understood. Colchicine does not lessen the production of uric acid by the body or increase the rate of elimination through the urine. Yet it has proved very effective in lessening the pain and distress of the disease. Early in the attack, one colchicine tablet given every hour for five hours may be sufficient to put the disease under control. In severe attacks longer medication may be necessary. *Prolonged use* of the drug will bring on its principal side reaction, gastrointestinal distress. When this happens the drug should be stopped.

RHEUMATIC FEVER

Rheumatic fever is not a heart disease, as so many people mistakenly believe. It *may* damage the heart.

Basically, rheumatic fever, like arthritis, is a rheumatic disease that in its early stages will affect the joints. For that matter, the initial symptoms of rheumatic fever are so like those of rheumatoid arthritis that in the early stages even the most skilled specialist finds it difficult to distinguish between the two. It is common practice to delay making a positive diagnosis until some additional symptoms develop.

It is said that rheumatic fever only "licks the joints but bites the heart." Conversely, rheumatoid arthritis only licks the heart but bites into the joints. Though the aches and pains of rheumatic fever may at times be quite severe, they will disappear entirely once the disease subsides. Should the disease flare up again, the joint symptoms will return. However, no joint damage will be left behind regardless of the number of attacks. Whatever damage is done—and this happens in only one case out of every three—will be done to the heart muscle.

Rheumatic fever is the most common cause of heart disease under the age of 40. It most often strikes children. However, it is not primarily a disease of childhood. The most striking proof of this is that during World War II more than 40,000 servicemen contracted the disease.

The exact incidence of rheumatic fever has been difficult to establish. It is estimated though that about one and one-third per cent of the children of school age in this country have the disease.

Watch out for infections

As with rheumatoid arthritis, the cause of rheumatic fever is not known. However, there appears to be a close relationship between it and a "strep" infection. That *streptococci*, disease-causing bacteria, are in some way associated with rheumatic fever is seen in the fact that the disease will often follow a "strep" throat or an attack of acute tonsillitis. Fortunately, only about three per cent of the general population suffering such infections come down with rheumatic fever.

Prevention is the most desirable treatment in rheumatic fever. For the seriousness of the disease is in the fact that once it has struck, you are subject to repeated attacks and with each attack there is continued damage to the heart. The chances are that one out of every two "strep" throats or infections will cause a recurrence of rheumatic fever if you have previously had the disease. Knowing, therefore, that a "strep" infection is essential to trigger a rheumatic fever attack, the *prevention of such infections* is of prime importance.

The continued use of either of two drugs in persons who have had rheumatic fever has proved most effective in preventing recurring attacks. The drugs are *penicillin* and *sulfadiazine*. Both can be used continually for an indefinite number of years.

The principal problem in treating an attack of rheumatic fever is the possible damage to the heart. To minimize the risk of such damage, complete bed rest is essential until all signs of disease activity have disappeared. In many cases, six to ten weeks of absolute rest in bed is sufficient, though at times several months or even a year or two may be necessary.

About the only activity permitted during this period of rest are trips to the toilet, and these must be in a wheel chair. In some cases not even this much activity is allowed. Daily doses of aspirin and the injection of prednisone are also a part of the treatment during the first month or two of the attack.

Along with rest and the use of drugs, good nursing care is necessary. During the acute stage a liquid or a semisolid diet is desirable. There should be an increase in the use of fluids to replace water lost by sweating. Soft pillows may be used to cushion inflamed joints.

When laboratory tests show the disease has remained subsided for at least two weeks and your general condition has improved satisfactorily, the *gradual* transition from bed rest to activity is begun.

There is no reason why a person who has had an attack of rheumatic fever should not be able to resume a normal and a fairly active life.

SHOULDER-HAND SYNDROME

Though in effect a form of rheumatism, the *shoulder-hand syndrome* has sufficient distinctive features to mark it as a separate ailment. The syndrome most often develops after a stroke, a heart attack, or a blood clot in a lung. In some instances, however, it will appear for no apparent reason at all and will be mistakenly diagnosed as rheumatoid arthritis, bursitis, or some other rheumatic disease. The basic cause is not known, although it is thought to be the result of a nutritional defect in certain nerves.

The principal feature of the syndrome is a swollen, tender, and painful shoulder accompanied by a similar condition in the hand on the same side of the body. Although usually only one side of the body is affected, both shoulders and both hands *may* be involved. The shoulder becomes so sensitive that motion is almost impossible. The hand becomes boggy and puffed and at times feels hot and sweaty. Motion in the hand is also restricted and painful.

In many cases, these symptoms will completely subside after several weeks, regardless of what the treatment may be. At times though, the ailment may become chronic and quite disabling. When this happens, the shoulder becomes stiff and motionless and the hand becomes cold and shrunken, with tightness limiting the use of the fingers.

The treatment of the shoulder-hand syndrome is varied and in general has not been too successful. Physical therapy (especially heat) and nerve-blocking drugs are used to allay the pain. Functional exercises are used to prevent stiffness and the loss of motion. In some cases unusually large doses of cortisone, far larger than those used in rheumatoid arthritis, may over a period of several weeks produce a marked benefit. ACTH is also used at times. Paraffin baths have proved helpful in easing the tightness of the hands. Keeping the arm elevated will sometimes prevent swelling of the hands.

The earlier the syndrome can be brought under control, the better are the chances of recovery and the less are the chances of permanent damage or of being left with some permanent stiffness in the shoulder and the hand.

INFECTIOUS ARTHRITIS

This arthritic condition is caused by *bacteria* that get into a joint, multiply, and create an infection. Many types of bacteria have been found to be responsible.

They may enter the joint through a wound or they may spread into the joint from a nearby local infection. In most instances, the bacteria are from some generalized infectious disease such as pneumonia or typhoid fever and are deposited in the joint by the blood stream. Usually, only one joint will be involved.

Infectious arthritis, at one time, was an extremely serious problem for which little could be done. As the infection within the joint grew and lingered on, the joint became hot, swollen, and tender. A large abscess often developed that not only caused severe pain and limited motion but also damaged the joint and at times led to crippling.

Now, with the availability of the potent *antibiotic* drugs, the various bacteria that cause this arthritic condition are often destroyed before any joint damage can be done. In most instances, the bacteria are killed during the normal course of treating the original infectious disease. Because there is always the danger that bacteria might cause irreparable damage to the joint lining, it is important that *all* infectious diseases be treated as promptly as possible. Once the infection is removed, the arthritis and the accompanying pain, discomfort, and disability will also disappear.

TRAUMATIC ARTHRITIS

This is a localized mechanical problem brought on by an injury to a particular joint. The injury may be due to a single incident, but more often it is caused by a series of minor injuries such as those experienced with occupational wear and tear.

Workers, for example, who day after day use powerful air hammers to break up asphalt streets or to chip barnacles off the bottoms of ships, may develop traumatic arthritis of the wrists. A man who makes his living laying tile floors may experience enough of a breakdown within his knees to bring on an arthritis attack. The baseball player who continually punishes the elbow of his throwing arm may develop traumatic arthritis in this joint. Overweight may also be a stress factor in damaging the hips or the many tiny joints in the feet.

Though such occupational stress is also a contributing factor in osteo-arthritis, the basic difference in traumatic arthritis is that aging and other body processes are not involved. Traumatic arthritis is purely and simply the breakdown of a joint that has been hurt or abused and as a result is *mechanically* impaired. There being no disease, only the injured joint is involved. The localized complaint does not spread to any other joints or parts of the body.

Rheumatoid arthritis, osteo-arthritis, rheumatic fever, gout, the shoulder-hand syndrome, infectious arthritis, and traumatic arthritis are the most common rheumatic diseases and together account for more than 95% of all the arthritis complaints seen by physicians.

RHEUMATISM

The most common of all rheumatic diseases, and, in a way, a form of arthritis, is that large group of varied and distressing conditions known as rheumatism. Most everyone during his lifetime has suffered from at least one attack of any number of these ailments that produce pain and stiffness in areas that do not particularly involve the joints. Some of the more common complaints are often referred to as nothing more than a stiff neck, stiff muscles, backache, side ache and the "charley horse" in the calf of the leg.

Rheumatism is the mildest of all rheumatic diseases. It is the inflammation of the connective tissue located outside the joints. Conversely, and in a broad sense, arthritis may be said to be rheumatism that has invaded the joint mechanism.

Rheumatism falls into two broad categories, organic and psychogenic. Organic rheumatism involves specific structures in the body and produces characteristic symptoms. Perhaps better known as non-articular (non-joint) rheumatism, it includes such ailments as:

Bursitis—The inflammation of a bursa, the flat fluid-filled cushion-like sac that prevents friction wherever in the body muscles, tendons and bone must work in crowded harmony. There are about 140 different bursae located in the human body and any one of these may become inflamed. The most common complaint is bursitis of the shoulder where the largest bursa is located. Inflammation of the bursa is associated with the injury of an adjacent tendon. More than 95% of the cases involving the shoulder are caused by occupational overuse of the arm over a period of time.

Tendonitis—The inflammation of a tendon, a fibrous cord of connective tissue in which the fibers of a muscle end and by which a muscle is attached to a bone or other structure. The ailment invariably is due to injury. As in bursitis, injury may be caused by a single episode such as a blow or it may follow a gradual breakdown of the tendon under the repeated stress of an extended series of apparently isolated minor incidents.

Tenosynovitis—Just as the tendon may become inflamed, so may the sheath in which it is encased be stricken. Here too, the most common cause is injury. As in tendonitis or bursitis, the injury may be severe and sudden or mild and repeated over a prolonged period. Tenosynovitis may also follow a specific infection and in some cases start for no apparent reason at all. At times, disease may cause a narrowing of the tendon sheath resulting in pain on motion.

Myositis—The inflammation of a muscle, commonly known as muscular rheumatism. The ailment may be acute or chronic and usually follows injury or strain, exposure to cold or dampness or a severe bout with some infectious disease. It usually comes on suddenly, the first signs being that of tenderness felt upon motion of an adjacent joint. The condition will often disappear within a few days. At times, though, it may continue to recur at frequent intervals or it may become chronic and linger on.

Fascitis—The fascia is a sheet or a band of fibrous tissue which blankets the body under the skin and also covers the muscles. When this dense layer of connective tissue becomes inflamed, it is known as fascitis. Though the condition may occur almost anywhere in the body, it is commonly seen only in the palms of the hands and the soles of the feet. This form of rhuematism is most disabling when it strikes the hands and indirectly involves the fingers. Its cause is unknown though injury and infection are often blamed.

Fibrositis—Inflammation of the fibrous tissue, another name for the connective tissue of the body. Yet, careful examination of samples of this tissue taken from persons suffering with the ailment has failed to detect any evidence of an active inflammatory process. One widely held theory is that fibrositis is caused by a chemical reaction within the fibrous tissue caused by everyday emotional tension. These chemical changes bring about aches, pain and general discomfort.

Psychogenic rheumatism, the other category of the ailment, is not a disease in the common sense of the word but a functional disorder. While interfering with muscle tissue, it causes no damage or destruction as do the many inflammatory forms of rheumatism, such as those referred to above. Though not an organic disease, it is nevertheless mighty real. It is not a psychosomatic disorder in which imagined ills bring on any number of unwarranted complaints. The distressing symptoms of the disease are all they are said to be; stiffness, tiredness and a general distressing ache that can be extremely unbearable.

Psychogenic rheumatism is a muscular reaction to stress and strain. It is, in a sense, muscle fatigue. Its basic ingredients are chronic fatigue and mental and physical unrest, the by-products of today's high pressured pace of living and the desire to keep abreast of the competition, socially and economically. It is the result of the tissues being forced to literally hum at fever pitch and collapsing with fatigue when they are no longer able to sustain the demands being made of them. The condition is seen primarily in tense, anxious and nervous individuals.

Most forms of rheumatism are rather mild. They do not provoke too much concern and are usually regarded as non-serious temporary distress due to being overtired, having a bad cold, being in a draft or perhaps receiving a minor bruise or an injury. A good many individuals suffering from rheumatism do not even bother visiting a physician. Rest and home remedies are usually the rule. When pain and discomfort become unbearable, medical advice is sought.

The treatment of rheumatism is directed at helping alleviate the symptoms of the ailment. This mainly consists of employing the measures of Home Care you will find detailed in Part One of this book. Quite often these physical therapy techniques, done in your own home with the supervision of your doctor, will be all that you will need to recover. In some instances, in addition to Home Care, your doctor may see fit to prescribe some specific form of therapy directed at the basic cause or contributing cause of your particular problem.

REMEMBER THESE POINTS
ABOUT THE LESS COMMON KINDS OF ARTHRITIS

✔ 1. Certain diseases, less common than rheumatoid and osteo, are classed in the arthritis category because they act like arthritis.

✔ 2. The most important of these are: gouty arthritis, rheumatic fever, the shoulder-hand syndrome, infectious arthritis, and traumatic arthritis.

✔ 3. Only one of these is really serious: the shoulder-hand syndrome. There is no reliable treatment for it. The others, fortunately, can be successfully treated with drugs.

✔ 4. Rheumatism is the most common and the mildest of all rheumatic diseases. Treatment is directed at the particular form of the ailment with rest and Home Care generally employed.

~~~ 13

QUICK ANSWERS
TO 101 BASIC
QUESTIONS

ARTHRITIS IS NOT A SIMPLE DISEASE. THE MANY FORMS IT
takes and the numerous ways in which it expresses itself are
sometimes enough to puzzle even the physicians in the field. Its
mixed-up nature has resulted in the accumulation of more no-
tions, superstitions, and misinformation than exist about any
other disease known today.

So it is quite understandable that you may have a question or
two about arthritis. The chances are that your questions are an-
swered in this chapter.

How was it possible to anticipate what questions could possibly arise in your mind? It wasn't difficult at all.

As part of its nation-wide program of public education, the

Arthritis and Rheumatism Foundation holds Public Health Forums under the sponsorship of its many Chapters about the country. Teams of the nation's leading arthritis specialists, the same whose scientific contributions are the basis for this book, speak at these forums. Thorough and explicit as the group of rheumatologists on the forum platform may be, there are always numerous questions that are asked by each audience afterwards. The following are the 101 questions—one for good measure—that have been asked most often at these arthritis forums.

1. Q. Should I move to a warmer climate?
   A. It is not advisable to endanger your economic status or disrupt your social ties in a vain effort to seek a climate that will cure your arthritis. You will do better to fight your problem at home with the aid of skilled medical supervision.

2. Q. Is physical therapy a cure for arthritis?
   A. Physical therapy alone is no cure, but it can be greatly effective toward partial or complete rehabilitation.

3. Q. Will I be crippled?
   A. Only a very small percentage of rheumatoid arthritics are in danger of crippling. However, deformities in most of these cases can be successfully prevented.

4. Q. What are my chances of recovery?
   A. Seven out of every 10 persons with crippling arthritis show marked improvement after proper medical care.

5. Q. Should I continue at my regular job?
   A. By all means, if your arthritis is not severe or disabling and your work does not aggravate your involved joints.

6. *Q.* Will arthritis cure itself without treatment?

   A. Yes, in some cases even of active rheumatoid arthritis. However, there is no way of identifying these cases in advance.

7. *Q.* If I rest too long in bed my joints seem to stiffen more.

   A. You may break up long sessions in bed with brief periods of limbering-up exercises.

8. *Q.* What about the patent medicines advertised for arthritis?

   A. These usually contain one of the salicylates such as aspirin and no matter how expensive do no more than provide the relief from pain, made possible by the low-cost aspirin they contain.

9. *Q.* Will the use of orange juice and cod liver oil "lubricate" the joints of a person suffering from arthritis?

   A. No, for these substances—or any other foods, for that matter—play no part in the lubrication of your joints.

10. *Q.* Are blood transfusions a cure for arthritis?

    A. No. However, should anemia develop, transfusions may be used to help bring the blood back to normal.

11. *Q.* Will the removal of one's teeth or tonsils cure arthritis?

    A. No. However, if your teeth are abscessed or your tonsils are infected, removal may lessen the strain upon your body's defenses and thus ease your joint aches and pains.

12. *Q.* Is arthritis hereditary?

    A. Some forms of arthritis seem to run in families. The tendency, though, is not strong enough to cause any arthritis sufferer to hesitate about getting married.

13. Q. Does heavy manual labor cause arthritis?
    A. It no doubt contributes to the onset of the disease
    but there is great doubt that it is a cause.

14. Q. Do children ever get arthritis?
    A. Children as young as eight months of age have been
    known to have rheumatoid arthritis.

15. Q. Is there a danger of getting diabetes from arthritis?
    A. Not from arthritis but from the use of cortisone and
    any of its derivatives.

16. Q. Will arthritis of the spine affect the brain?
    A. No. The ailment is confined to the joints of the
    spinal column.

17. Q. How do you distinguish arthritis from dystrophy?
    A. Arthritis is a progressive inflammation of the joints;
    muscular dystrophy is a wasting away of the mus-
    cles.

18. Q. Can calcium be removed from joints successfully?
    A. Yes, surgical and other techniques are available
    when necessary.

19. Q. Is it safe to take salicylates for an indefinite length
    of time?
    A. Generally, yes. They are the safest of all the drugs
    used in the treatment of arthritis and usually are
    prescribed first.

20. Q. Does aspirin cure arthritis?
    A. Aspirin and the other salicylates are able to reduce
    pain and inflammation but have no affect on the
    disease process.

21. Q. How do you determine the kind of arthritis you
    have?

A. Only a doctor can do this. Distinguishing among the various forms of arthritis can sometimes be quite tricky.

22. Q. Can anybody go to an Arthritis Clinic?
    A. It depends upon the rules set up by the medical institution in which the clinic is located.

23. Q. Are iodides used in the treatment of arthritis?
    A. Though from time to time their use is popular, there is no specific or unusual benefit to be derived from them.

24. Q. Is bee venom used to cure arthritis?
    A. Not any more. Suggested many years ago, this form of therapy produces so few beneficial results that it has long been discontinued as of no value.

25. Q. Are there any vaccines for the treatment of arthritis?
    A. None is now in use. The one-time belief in vaccines no longer exists.

26. Q. Will hormones retard the aging of the joints?
    A. No. In some patients they have led to bone destruction.

27. Q. Will alfalfa tea relieve arthritis pains?
    A. If you think it does, then it can only be mental. Horses eat alfalfa all their lives and yet have arthritis.

28. Q. Does a constant buzzing in my ears have anything to do with arthritis?
    A. No. It is not a symptom of arthritis nor does it mean that you are going to get the disease.

29. Q. Are dry skin, scalp, and ears symptoms of arthritis?
    A. No.

30. Q. Is premature graying of the hair caused by arthritis?
    A. No.

31. Q. Are varicose veins or tingling of the extremities signs of arthritis?
    A. No.

32. Q. My joints are stiff in the morning. Do I have arthritis?
    A. Morning stiffness may be an early sign of arthritis, but not necessarily. Other symptoms must also be present.

33. Q. Do the oils in food help lubricate the joints?
    A. No, oils and fats are not involved in the substances that lubricate the joints.

34. Q. Does the way you eat influence the deposit of calcium in joints?
    A. No. The way in which calcium is used by the body in building bones has nothing to do with how it is eaten.

35. Q. Does the drinking of water make arthritis worse?
    A. There is no scientific evidence that drinking water has any effect at all upon arthritis.

36. Q. Are iodine foods of value in arthritis?
    A. There is no scientific evidence to suggest that iodine will help arthritis or any other rheumatic disease.

37. Q. Does Vitamin D stimulate the adrenal glands to make cortisone?
    A. Cortisone and the other adrenal steroids are produced from very simple substances. Vitamin D plays no part in their production.

38. Q. Does the person with arthritis produce less cortisone than a person without the disease?
    A. Studies indicate no difference.

39. Q. Is the cortisone in a normal person stronger than the hormone in an arthritic person?
    A. There is no special type of cortisone produced in the person with arthritis.

40. Q. Is there any relationship between constipation and arthritis?
    A. None whatsoever. There is no such diagnosis as "chronic constipated arthritis" as believed by many persons.

41. Q. Are gold salts of value in the treatment of arthritis?
    A. Yes, but only in the rheumatoid form of the disease.

42. Q. What is myositis?
    A. The inflammation of a muscle.

43. Q. Are simple muscle pains a symptom of arthritis?
    A. Probably not. Not all aches and pains mean arthritis.

44. Q. Is it a waste of time to use liniments for arthritis?
    A. A lamp is a far more efficient way of producing beneficial heat.

45. Q. Does cracking or snapping of a joint mean arthritis?
    A. Many people are able to crack their joints, a sound caused by the slipping of tendons or ligaments over the end of a bone, yet have no joint disease.

46. Q. Do not arthritic joints make noise?
    A. Some do. In rheumatoid arthritis, granulation tissue in a joint may cause a rubbing sound. A course grating or grinding sound is often more felt than heard in osteo-arthritis.

47. Q. I have backaches. Do they mean arthritis?
    A. There are about 85 different causes of backache, including arthritis. Check with your doctor.

48. Q. Does the arthritis patient have poor circulation?
    A. Perhaps not in the common usage of the phrase. However, there is indication that circulation is impaired in arthritic joints.

49. Q. What causes the swelling in arthritis?
    A. Usually, the presence of abnormally large amounts of fluid.

50. Q. What causes arthritic fingers to curl up?
    A. Destruction of the joints that results in a union of bony parts, along with a wasting of ligaments and muscles.

51. Q. X rays show osteo-arthritis at the base of my spine. What kind of treatment shall I take?
    A. Almost everyone past middle life shows degenerative changes at the base of the spine. Unless symptoms are present no treatment is indicated.

52. Q. Is there a treatment for osteo-arthritis of the spine?
    A. The same as for osteo-arthritis elsewhere. Rest, heat, and aspirin.

53. Q. Does high humidity cause discomfort in arthritis?
    A. Humidity seems to have a definite effect upon the symptoms of many arthritics. Most arthritics feel better on hot dry days or on cold dry days and worse on hot humid days or on cold damp days.

54. Q. Is B-12 beneficial for arthritis?
    A. It has proved unsuccessful in rheumatoid arthritis though some persons with osteo-arthritis believe it has helped them.

55. Q. Does constant tiredness or listlessness mean arthritis?
    A. Constant fatigue of body and mind is considered to be a frequent precursor of rheumatoid arthritis.

56. Q. Why is arthritis worse in the morning?
    A. Prolonged rest seems to jell the joints.

57. Q. What can be done for stiff finger joints?
    A. Heat and exercise as prescribed by your doctor should help.

58. Q. Will a Vitamin A diet cure arthritis?
    A. The idea of Vitamin A deficiency in rheumatoid arthritis has been generally discarded. Treatment with it has proved to be unsuccessful.

59. Q. Are multiple vitamins good for arthritis?
    A. Not for arthritis but good for your general body health, if your doctor finds that you need vitamin supplements.

60. Q. Are food supplements good for arthritis?
    A. They are only good to improve your general health if it is below par. They will do your arthritis no direct good.

61. Q. Is a poor appetite a sign of arthritis?
    A. Along with a gradual loss of weight and anemia, it is.

62. Q. Does evening thirst and general distress mean arthritis?
    A. If this combination is associated with the low-grade fever that may persist for months during active rheumatoid arthritis.

63. Q. Can a back bent by arthritis be straightened?
    A. Casts, braces, strappings, and surgery are used.

64. Q. Is proper diet the best path to cure osteo-arthritis?
    A. If you are overweight and the added weight is aggravating your involved joints.

65. Q. Does the weather affect arthritis?
    A. It does influence the severity of the aches and pains.

66. Q. Does excessive tension affect arthritis?
    A. Persons with the disease seem to feel worse when under some emotional strain.

67. Q. Is it possible to have arthritis in your head?
    A. Not in your brain but in your jaw, which has the only joints in your head.

68. Q. Is ultrasonic therapy a cure for arthritis?
    A. It is another way of providing internal heat; but it is not a cure.

69. Q. Would a vibrator help arthritis?
    A. The action of vibrators is too severe for tender joints.

70. Q. Will my being overweight prohibit the use of cortisone?
    A. It may, as the drug is known to cause diabetes.

71. Q. Is cortisone perfectly safe?
    A. It is a highly toxic drug that must be handled with care and can be taken only by a small percentage of rheumatoid arthritics.

72. Q. What is the current recommended treatment for arthritis?
    A. Aspirin, physical medicine, and home care.

73. Q. Should the arthritic give in to pain, or should he keep going?
    A. Neither. Pain can be put under control. Forcing yourself to keep going will often further aggravate your ailment.

74. Q. If pregnancy helps ease the pains of arthritis, then why did I get arthritis when I was five months pregnant?

A. Pregnancy sometimes brings on arthritis too.

75. Q. Is arthritis emotional in origin?
   A. In some people an emotional upheaval can trigger an arthritis attack.

76. Q. Does tuberculosis of the joints have anything to do with arthritis?
   A. The TB infection may result in an arthritic condition.

77. Q. Is arthritis ever fatal?
   A. It seldom is. Arthritis itself is a chronic disease.

78. Q. Does arthritis ever go away?
   A. Yes, in time it burns itself out.

79. Q. Will crippling caused by arthritis correct itself?
   A. No. The wasting away of the joints, the destruction of the cartilage, and the thinning of the involved bones cannot be repaired.

80. Q. What joints are most often crippled by arthritis?
   A. Those of the hands and the fingers.

81. Q. What are the most oft-ignored warning signs of arthritis?
   A. The slight joint swellings that come and go over the years.

82. Q. Are there any tests for arthritis?
   A. A blood test is now being perfected. However, there are no generally useful diagnostic tests that can be compared to the tests for diabetes or tuberculosis.

83. Q. Can crippling be predicted in advance?
   A. No. A method for determining this is something doctors have been looking for for many years.

84. Q. Is rheumatoid arthritis a crippling disease?

A. The threat of severe crippling always exists but is known in only about 20% of the cases.

85. Q. Is arthritis a disease of old age?
A. Rheumatoid arthritis may strike at any age, though osteo-arthritis seldom is seen in persons under 40.

86. Q. Is there any one age at which most arthritis starts?
A. There is no accurate indication of when the disease actually starts. Arthritis is insidious and may be slowly smoldering beneath the surface for years before it breaks out.

87. Q. Do more women get arthritis than men?
A. Only when rheumatoid arthritis is concerned. The reason is not entirely clear, though the female hormonal structure may be implicated.

88. Q. Is pregnancy a cure for rheumatoid arthritis?
A. No. After the birth of the baby the symptoms usually return.

89. Q. Can I prevent rheumatoid arthritis?
A. There are no sure measures. The precipitating causes that bring on the disease are too common or not sufficiently specific to be readily controlled.

90. Q. Can I lessen the chances of getting rheumatoid arthritis?
A. If you try to live free of everyday tensions and anxieties, get sufficient rest and sleep, and avoid exposure to dampness and cold, you may.

91. Q. If I go to bed for several months will I cure my arthritis?
A. Rest can be overdone. Prolonged bed rest not balanced by therapeutic exercise will weaken and waste

your muscles, thus limiting motion and making crippling more severe.

92. Q. Is there a medicine to cure arthritis?
    A. No. There is no known cure for the disease.

93. Q. Is arthritis a modern disease?
    A. No. The pressure of modern living perhaps has helped increase the incidence of the disease. Fossilized remains of prehistoric reptiles show definite signs of arthritis.

94. Q. Is rheumatoid arthritis strictly a disease of the joints?
    A. Though it does involve the joints, it may also involve one or more organs of the body. Actually, it is a disease of the entire body.

95. Q. Is osteo-arthritis solely a disease of aging?
    A. There is some relationship between osteo-arthritis and advancing age, though there is evidence that other factors may be involved.

96. Q. What is the cure for osteo-arthritis?
    A. There isn't any. Neither is there any specific treatment. The condition is managed by the control of symptoms and the relief of strain upon the affected joints.

97. Q. Does rheumatoid arthritis come on suddenly?
    A. It may, but more often it comes on gradually.

98. Q. Can the ordinary family doctor diagnose arthritis properly?
    A. Yes, he should be able to.

99. Q. Is it possible to stop rheumatoid arthritis?
    A. The progress of the disease may be interrupted

temporarily or permanently at any stage. No patient is beyond aid.

100. Q. What is the first treatment an arthritis doctor gives?
     A. He puts the arthritic patient in as good general health as is possible, using rest and an adequately nutritious diet.

101. Q. Will the wearing of proper shoes lessen the aches and pains of osteo-arthritis?
     A. Foot disorders often transmit undue stress upward, producing damaging effects on many joints. Improve foot mechanics and wear properly fitted shoes and you'll relieve the pain due to osteo-arthritis.

~~~ 14

WHERE YOU CAN GO FOR HELP

THIS CHAPTER IS A LIST OF ALL THE CLINICS IN THE UNITED States that specialize in the treatment of arthritis. They are listed alphabetically, first by state and then by city.

The list was compiled by the Arthritis and Rheumatism Foundation. An asterisk (*) in front of the name of a clinic means that the Foundation is not sure of the present status of the clinic. If you are interested, you should verify by a letter to that particular clinic.

The information is arranged like this: Name of clinic, address, doctor in charge, whether it is free or pay, what the entrance requirements are, if any.

223

ALABAMA

BIRMINGHAM:
Jefferson-Hillman Hospital
619 South 19th Street
Dr. J. O. Finney in charge.
Free and part pay clinic.
Restricted to residents of Jefferson County.

ARIZONA

PHOENIX:
*Arthritis Clinic
1313 North 2nd Street
Dr. W. A. Bishop in charge.

TUCSON:
Pima County Hospital
Dr. Harold J. Rowe in charge.
Free clinic.
Restricted to medically indigent residents of Pima County for at least one year.

ARKANSAS

HOT SPRINGS:
Leo N. Levi Memorial Hospital
320 Prospect Avenue
Dr. O. C. Wenger in charge.
Free clinic.
No geographical restrictions.

CALIFORNIA

BERKELEY:
Herrick Memorial Hospital
2001 Dwight Way

Dr. Edwin B. McLean in charge.
Part pay clinic.
No geographical restrictions.

FRESNO:
Fresno County General Hospital
4475 E. Ventura Avenue
Dr. Leopold Snyder in charge.
Free clinic.
Restricted to residents of Fresno County.

LOS ANGELES:
Los Angeles County General Hospital
1200 North State Street
Dr. Carlos F. Sacasa in charge.
Free and part pay (indigent patients only).
Restricted to residents of Los Angeles County.

Orthopedic Hospital
2400 South Flower Street
Dr. A. Brockway in charge.
Free and part pay clinic.
No geographical restrictions.

Cedars of Lebanon Hospital
4833 Fountain Avenue
Dr. H. S. Weinberger in charge.
Free and part pay clinic.
No geographical restrictions.

White Memorial Hospital
321 North Boyle Avenue
Dr. Fred B. Moor in charge.

Part pay clinic.
No geographical restrictions.

Children's Hospital
4614 Sunset Boulevard
Dr. Mary Malloy in charge.
Free and part pay clinic.
Restricted to residents of Los
Angeles County.

Wadsworth Veterans Administration
Veterans Administration Center
Dr. Howard J. Weinberger in charge.
Free for service connected cases.
Charges for non-service connected disability cases.
For veterans only.

Good Hope Clinic
1241 Shatto
Dr. Richard D. Miller in charge.
Part pay clinic.
Restricted to residents of Los
Angeles County (with exceptions).

Methodist Hospital of Southern California
2826 So. Hope Street
Dr. Daniel Beltz in charge.
Pay clinic.
No geographical restrictions.

OAKLAND:
Highland Alameda County
Hospital

2701 14th Avenue.
Dr. Robert S. Peers in charge.
Free clinic.
Restricted to Alameda County
residents.

PASADENA:
Pasadena Dispensary
38 Congress Street
Drs. Miller and Schlueter in charge.
Part pay clinic.
Restricted to residents of Pasadena, S. Pasadena, Altadena
and San Marino.

SAN DIEGO:
San Diego County General
Hospital
Dr. Lincoln W. Cromwell in charge.
Free clinic.
Restricted to residents of San
Diego County.

SAN FRANCISCO:
Mt. Zion Hospital, OPD
1600 Divisadero St.
Dr. Ephraim P. Engleman and
Dr. Morris R. Gordon in charge.
Free clinic.
Restricted to residents of San
Francisco.

St. Mary's Hospital
2200 Hayes Street
Dr. John M. Elliot in charge.

SAN FRANCISCO (continued):
Pay clinic.
No geographical restrictions.

San Francisco Polyclinic
1055 Pine Street
Dr. William C. Kuzell in
charge.
Part pay clinic.
No geographical restrictions.

Stanford University School of
Medicine
2398 Sacramento Street
Dr. Roland A. Davison in
charge.
Pay clinic.
No geographical restrictions.

University of California Hospital
Third and Parnassus Avenues
Dr. Stacy R. Mettier in charge.
Free and part pay clinic.
No geographical restrictions.

Veterans Administration Regional Office
49 Fourth Street
Dr. Ephraim P. Engleman in
charge.
Free to veterans (out-patients).

Veterans Administration Hospital
42nd and Clement Streets
Dr. Ephraim F. Engleman in
charge.
Free to veterans (in-patients).

SANTA BARBARA:
Santa Barbara General Hospital
Dr. Benjamin H. Huggins in
charge.
Part pay clinic.
Restricted to residents of Santa
Barbara County.

SAN JOSE:
Santa Clara County Hospital
Los Gatos Road
Dr. Joseph E. Giansiracusa in
charge.
Free clinic.
Restricted to residents of Santa
Clara County.

SAN LEANDRO:
Fairmont Hospital of Alameda
County
15400 Foothill Boulevard
Dr. Robert S. Peers in charge.
Free clinic.
Restricted to residents of lower Alameda County.

COLORADO
DENVER:
University of Colorado Medical Center
4200 East 9th Avenue
Dr. Charley J. Smyth in charge.
Free and part pay.
Restricted to residents of Colorado.

CONNECTICUT

BRIDGEPORT:
  City Dispensary
  835 Washington Avenue
  Dr. Hardenburgh in charge.
  Part pay (50¢).
  No geographical restrictions.

HARTFORD:
  Hartford Dispensary
  59 Winthrop Street
  Dr. Harold S. Backus in charge.
  Restricted to indigent patients
    of Hartford County.

  McCook Memorial Hospital
  2 Holcomb Street
  Dr. Edward Scull in charge.
  Part pay clinic.
  Restricted to residents of
    Greater Hartford.

  Hartford Hospital
  80 Seymour Street
  Drs. George Wulp, Joseph J.
    Lankin and Edward Scull in
    charge.
  Part pay clinic.
  Referral by doctor, through
    diagnostic clinic.

NEW HAVEN:
  Grace-New Haven Community
    Hospital
  789 Howard Avenue
  Dr. Gideon K. deForest in
    charge.
  Part pay.

Patients outside New Haven
  must be referred by doctor
  and pay maximum fee.

DELAWARE

WILMINGTON:
  Delaware Hospital
  14th and Washington Street
  Dr. Arthur J. Heather in
    charge.
  Free and part pay.
  No geographical restrictions.

DISTRICT OF COLUMBIA

George Washington Univer-
  sity Hospital
901 23rd Street, N.W.
Dr. Thomas McP. Brown in
  charge.
Part pay.
Restricted to Washington,
  D.C. and Metropolitan area.

Georgetown University Hospital
3800 Reservoir Road
Dr. Darrell C. Crain in charge.
Free and part pay.
Restricted to Metropolitan
  area of District of Columbia,
  nearby Maryland and Virginia.

*Rheumatology Clinic
  Mount Alto Hospital

DISTRICT OF COLUMBIA
(continued):
Dr. Thomas McP. Brown in
charge.
For local veterans.

*Walter Reed Hospital
Dr. Darrell C. Crain in charge.
For the army.

FLORIDA

JACKSONVILLE:
Duval Medical Center
Dr. Walker Stamps in charge.
Free clinic.
Restricted to indigent patients
of Duval County, Florida.

GEORGIA

ATLANTA:
Grady Memorial Hospital
36 Butler Street
Dr. Harold L. Murray in
charge.
Free clinic.
Restricted to residents of Ful-
ton and DeKalb counties.

*City Charity Hospital

*Lawson Veterans Hospital
Dr. Max Michael in charge.

ILLINOIS

CHICAGO:
Mercy Hospital
2537 Prairie Avenue
Dr. Stanley Fahlstrom in
charge.

Free and part pay.
No geographical restrictions.

Northwestern University Medical School Clinics
303 East Chicago Avenue
Dr. H. H. Kilgore in charge.
Free and part pay.
Restricted to residents of Chicago.

Central Free Dispensary at
Presbyterian Hospital
1748 W. Harrison Street
Dr. W. G. Hibbs in charge.
Free and part pay.
Limits: 22nd Street on South;
Canal Street on East; Fulton
Street on North; and City
Limits on West.

Cook County Hospital
1825 Harrison Street
Dr. Eugene Traut in charge.
Free clinic.
Restricted to residents of Cook
County.

Michael Reese Hospital
Mandel Clinic
Free and part pay.
Restricted to indigent residents
of Chicago.

Mount Sinai Hospital
15th and California
Dr. Edward Rosenberg in
charge.
Free and part pay.
Restricted to residents of Chicago.

Grant Hospital of Chicago
551 Grant Place
Dr. Joseph E. Allegretti in
charge.
Free and part pay.
Restricted to residents north
of Madison Street, Chicago.

University of Chicago Clinics
950 East 59th Street
Dr. Delbert M. Bergenstal in
charge.
Part pay.
No geographical restrictions.

*Provident Hospital
5034 South Vincennes

*University of Illinois Clinic
1819 West Polk Street

*Veterans Administration Hos-
pital
366 West Adams Street

*Montgomery Ward Clinic
747 North Fairbanks Court

INDIANA
INDIANAPOLIS:
*Indianapolis General Hospital
960 Locke Street

KENTUCKY
LOUISVILLE:
Louisville General Hospital
323 E. Chestnut Street
Dr. Robert L. McClendon in
charge.

Free and part pay.
Restricted to residents of
Louisville and Jefferson
County, Kentucky.

LOUISIANA
NEW ORLEANS:
Tulane Arthritis Clinic
Hutchinson Memorial Build-
ing
Tulane Medical School
1430 Tulane Avenue
Dr. Maridel Saunders in
charge.
Free clinic.
Limited to patients eligible for
charity care.

MAINE
BANGOR:
Eastern Maine General Hos-
pital
489 State Street
Dr. Robert Kellogg in charge.
Free clinic.
No geographical restrictions.

PORTLAND:
*Maine General Hospital
22 Arsenal Street

WATERVILLE:
*Thayer Hospital
214 Maine Street

MARYLAND

ANNAPOLIS:
Anne Arundel General Hospital
Dr. Harry Klinefelter in charge.
Free clinic.
Restricted to residents of Anne Arundel County.

BALTIMORE:
Sinai Hospital
Monument & Rutland Streets
Dr. Herbert N. Gundersheimer, Jr., in charge.
Free and part pay.

Baltimore City Hospital
4840 Eastern Avenue
Dr. Joseph J. Bunim in charge.
Free and part pay.

University of Maryland
Redwood and Greene Streets
Dr. Leon A. Kochman in charge.
Free clinic.
Restricted to residents of Baltimore.

*Johns Hopkins University Hospital
Broadway and Monument Street

CAMBRIDGE:
Cambridge-Maryland Hospital
Dr. Charles W. Wainwright in charge.
Free clinic.

CENTREVILLE:
Arthritis Clinic
Dr. Charles W. Wainwright in charge.
Free clinic.
Restricted to residents of Queen Anne's county.

CHESTERTOWN:
Kent and Queen Anne Hospital
Dr. R. W. Farr in charge.
Restricted to residents of Kent County.

CHEVERLY:
Prince George's General Hospital
Dr. Leon A. Kochman in charge.
Free clinic.
No geographical restrictions.

CUMBERLAND:
Memorial Hospital
Dr. Leon A. Kochman in charge.
Part pay clinic.
No geographical restrictions.

ELKTON:
Union Hospital
Dr. Charles W. Wainwright in charge.
Free clinic.
No geographical restrictions.

ELLICOTT CITY:
Howard County Health Dept.

Dr. Leon A. Kochman in charge.
Free clinic.
No geographical restrictions.

FREDERICK:
Frederick County Health Dept.
12 East Church Street
Dr. Leon A. Kochman in charge.
Free clinic.
Restricted to residents of Frederick County.

HAVRE DE GRACE:
Harford County Health Dept.
Dr. Harry F. Klinefelter in charge.
Free clinic.
Restricted to residents of Harford County.

LEONARDTOWN:
*Dr. Alan D. Houser
Deputy State Health Officer
St. Mary's County.

OAKLAND:
*Dr. Thomas B. Dunne
Deputy State Health Officer
Garrett County.

POCOMOKE CITY:
*Dr. F. S. Waesche
Deputy State Health Officer
Worcester County.

SALISBURY:
Wicomico County Health Dept.
Dr. Charles W. Wainwright in charge.
Free clinic.
No geographical restrictions.

WESTMINSTER:
*Dr. W. Rose Cameron
County Health Officer
Carroll County.

MASSACHUSETTS

BOSTON:
Peter Bent Brigham Hospital
721 Huntington Avenue
Dr. Theodore Bayles in charge.
Free and part pay clinic.
Free only to residents of Suffolk County.

Boston Dispensary
25 Bennet Street
Dr. H. G. Brugsch in charge.
Free and part pay.
No geographical restrictions.

Massachusetts General Hospital
Dr. Walter Bauer in charge.
Part pay clinic.
No geographical restrictions.

Robert B. Brigham Hospital
125 Parker Hill Avenue
Dr. Sydney Stillman in charge.
Free and part pay clinic.
Free only to residents of Greater Metropolitan Boston.

BOSTON (continued):
Beth Israel Hospital
330 Brookline Avenue
Dr. Maurice Abrams in charge.
Full pay, part pay, and free.
No geographical restrictions.

House of the Good Samaritan
25 Binney Street
Dr. Howard B. Sprague in charge.
Clinic is primarily for rheumatic fever.

Carney Hospital
South Boston
Dr. Francis Colpoys in charge.
Part pay clinic.
No geographical restrictions.

*New England Medical Center

BRIGHTON:
St. Elizabeth's Hospital
736 Cambridge Street
Dr. Francis Colpoys in charge.
Part pay clinic.
No geographical restrictions.

CAMBRIDGE:
*Holy Ghost Hospital

HOLYOKE:
Skinner Clinic
Holyoke Hospital
Dr. Hans Waine in charge.
Free clinic.
No geographical restrictions.

LYNN:
Lynn Hospital
212 Boston Street

Dr. James D. C. Gowans in charge.
Part pay clinic.
No geographical restrictions.

PITTSFIELD:
Pittsfield General Hospital
Dr. F. K. Paddock in charge.
Part pay clinic.
No geographical restrictions.

SPRINGFIELD:
The Springfield Hospital
759 Chestnut Street
Dr. Eugene Walker in charge.
Part pay clinic.
Restricted to Agawam, East Longmeadow, Longmeadow, Springfield, W. Springfield, and Wilbraham.

WORCESTER:
Memorial Hospital
Belmont Street
Dr. S. Bachrach in charge.
Part pay clinic.
No geographical restrictions.

Worcester City Hospital
Dr. Leonard L. Tormey in charge.
Free clinic.
Restricted to residents of Worcester.

MICHIGAN

ANN ARBOR:
University (of Michigan) Hospital

1313 Ann Street
Dr. William D. Robinson in charge.
Part pay clinic.
No geographical restrictions, but must be referred to hospital by family physician.

DETROIT:
Henry Ford Hospital
Dr. Dwight C. Ensign in charge.
Part pay clinic.
No geographical restrictions.

Harper Hospital
3825 Brush Street
Dr. Joseph A. Rourke, Director.
Part pay clinic.
Restricted to residents of Metropolitan Detroit.

The Grace Hospital
Out-patient Department
Dr. T. M. Batchelor in charge.
Part pay clinic.
Restricted to residents of Metropolitan Detroit.

*Providence Hospital

*Detroit Receiving Hospital

*Mount Carmel Hospital

MINNESOTA
MINNEAPOLIS:
University of Minnesota Clinics
Drs. Paul J. Bilka and M.

Wetherby, co-directors.
Free and part pay clinic.
No geographical limitations.

MISSOURI
KANSAS CITY:
General Hospital #1
24th and Cherry Streets
Dr. C. Stewart Gillmor in charge.
Free and part pay clinic.
Limited to residents of Kansas City.

ST. LOUIS:
Saint Louis City Hospital
1515 Lafayette Avenue
Dr. Henry Rosenfeld in charge.
Free for indigent individuals.
Restricted to residents of the city of St. Louis for one year.

St. Louis City Hospital
Out-patient clinic
1600 South 14th Street
Dr. Henry Rosenfeld in charge.
Free clinic.
Restricted to city residents.

Barnes Hospital
600 South Kingshighway
Dr. Paul O. Hagemann in charge.
Free and part pay.
No geographical restrictions.

Firmin Desloge Hospital
1325 S. Grand Boulevard
Dr. R. O. Muether in charge.

St. Louis (continued):
Free and part pay.
Restricted to St. Louis County for free patients—no restrictions for paying patients.

St. Luke's Hospital
5535 Delmar Boulevard
Dr. Paul O. Hagemann in charge.
Free and part pay.
Restricted to residents of St. Louis and St. Louis county.

Jewish Hospital
216 South Kingshighway
Dr. Herman Meyer in charge.
Free and part pay.
No geographical restrictions.

*Arthritis Clinic
Wall Building
Drs. Henry and Herman Rosenfeld
Private clinic.

NEBRASKA
Omaha:
University of Nebraska Hospital
42nd Street and Dewey Avenue
Dr. Willson B. Moody in charge.
Free clinic.
Restricted to residents of state of Nebraska.

Creighton University
14th and Davenport Streets

Dr. H. N. Neu in charge.
Free clinic.
No geographical restrictions.

*Dr. F. Lowell Dunn
737 Medical Arts Building

NEW HAMPSHIRE
Hanover:
Mary Hitchcock Memorial Hospital
Dr. Joshua B. Burnett in charge.
Part pay clinic.
No geographical restrictions.

Manchester:
Elliot Hospital
Dr. V. C. Bragg in charge.
Part pay clinic.
No geographical restrictions.

NEW JERSEY
Atlantic City:
Atlantic City Hospital
26 South Ohio
Dr. C. B. Whims in charge.
Free clinic.
No geographical restrictions.

Hackensack:
Hackensack Hospital
Hackensack Place
Drs. Thompson and Denson in charge.
Part pay clinic.
Restricted to residents of Bergen County.

IRVINGTON:
*Irvington General Hospital
832 Chancellor Avenue

JERSEY CITY:
*Jersey City Medical Center
100 Clifton Place

MORRISTOWN:
Morristown Memorial Hospital
Dr. T. R. Failmezger in charge.
Free clinic.
No geographical restrictions.

All Souls Hospital
Dr. T. R. Failmezger in charge.
Free clinic.
No geographical restrictions.

NEWARK:
Newark Beth Israel Hospital
201 Lyons Avenue
Dr. Herman Tillis in charge.
Free and part pay.
No geographical restrictions.

Clara Maass Memorial Hospital
16—12th Avenue
Dr. Jacob Heyman in charge.
Part pay clinic.
No geographical restrictions.

Regional office
Veterans Administration
Dr. Irving L. Sperling in charge.
Free to veterans in New Jersey.

Hospital of St. Barnabas
685 High Street
Dr. John W. Gray in charge.
Part pay clinic.
No geographical restrictions.

*Lutheran Memorial Hospital
16—12th Avenue

*Presbyterian Hospital
27 South 9th Street

ORANGE:
New Jersey Orthopedic Hospital
179 Lincoln Avenue
Dr. J. W. Gray in charge.
Free and part pay.
No geographical restrictions.

TRENTON:
William McKinley Memorial Hospital
Brunswich Avenue
Dr. Peter J. Warter in charge.
Free and part pay clinic.
No geographical restrictions.

NEW MEXICO

ALBUQUERQUE:
Lovelace Clinic
4800 Gibson
Dr. C. M. Kemper in charge.
Pay clinic.
No geographical restrictions.

Arthritis Clinic
Community Health Center
Dr. S. W. Adler in charge.

TRUTH OR CONSEQUENCES:
*Carrie Tingley Hospital for Crippled Children

NEW YORK

ALBANY:

Albany Hospital
New Scotland Avenue
Dr. Thomas Frawley in charge.
Part pay clinic.
No geographical restrictions.

BRONX:

Fordham Hospital
Southern Boulevard
Dr. Leon Paris in charge.
Free clinic.
Geographical restrictions.

Montifiore Hospital
East Gunhill Road and Bainbridge Avenue
Dr. Karl Harpuder in charge.
Part pay.
Geographical restrictions.

Morrisania City Hospital
Walton Avenue and 168th Street
Dr. Fred Levy in charge.
Free clinic.
Geographical restrictions.

Lincoln Hospital
Concord Avenue and 141th Street
Dr. Benjamin E. Krentz in charge.
Free clinic.
Geographical restrictions.

BROOKLYN:

Greenpoint Hospital
Kingsland Avenue
Dr. Rubin Klein in charge.
Free clinic.
Geographical restrictions.

St. John's Episcopal Hospital
480 Herkimer Street
Dr. Felix Taubman and Dr. Bernard H. Perlman in charge.
Part pay clinic.
Geographical restrictions.

Cumberland Hospital
Auburn Place
Dr. Milton A. Wald in charge.
Free clinic.
Geographical restrictions.

The Brooklyn Hospital
DeKalb Avenue and Ashland Place
Dr. A. Sidney Barritt, Jr., in charge.
Part pay.
Geographical restrictions.

Long Island College Hospital
Henry Street
Dr. Julius E. Stolfi in charge.
Part pay.
Geographical restrictions.

Jewish Hospital of Brooklyn
555 Prospect Place
Dr. Abraham S. Gordon in charge.
Part pay.
Geographical restrictions.

Kings County Hospital, University Division
451 Clarkson Avenue
Dr. Charles M. Plotz in charge.
Free clinic.
Geographical restrictions.

Kings County Hospital, Open Division
451 Clarkson Avenue
Dr. Abraham S. Gordon in charge.
Free clinic.
Geographical restrictions.

Beth El Hospital
Linden Blvd. & Rockaway Parkway
Dr. Mendel Jacobi in charge.
Part pay clinic.
Geographical restrictions.

Maimonides Hospital
(Israel Zion Division)
4802 Tenth Avenue
Dr. Charles M. Plotz in charge.
Part pay clinic.
Geographical restrictions.

BUFFALO:
Buffalo General Hospital
100 High Street
Dr. L. Maxwell Lockie in charge.
Free and part pay clinic.
No geographical restrictions.

Buffalo Children's Hospital
219 Bryant Street
Dr. L. Maxwell Lockie in charge.

Free and part pay.
No geographical restrictions.

Edward J. Meyer Memorial Hospital
462 Grider Street
Dr. Harold Robins in charge.
Free and part pay clinic.
Restricted to residents of Erie County, except by special approval.

JAMAICA:
Queens General Hospital
164th Street and Grand Central Parkway
Dr. Louis W. Granirer in charge.
Free clinic.
Geographical restrictions.

Mary Immaculate Hospital
152-11 89th Avenue
Drs. Jeptha R. MacFarlane and Louis T. Cornacchia in charge.
Part pay clinic.
Geographical restrictions.

MANHATTAN:
Edward Daniels Faulkner Clinic
Presbyterian Hospital
622 West 168th Street
Dr. Charles Ragan in charge.
Part pay clinic.
Geographical restrictions.

Jewish Memorial Hospital
Broadway and 196th Street

MANHATTAN (continued):
Dr. Leo Braun in charge.
Part pay clinic.
Geographical restrictions.

Knickerbocker Hospital
70 Convent Avenue
Dr. LeMoyne C. Kelly in charge.
Part pay clinic.
Geographical restrictions.

Hospital for Joint Diseases
1919 Madison Avenue
Dr. Otto Steinbrocker in charge.
Part pay clinic.
Geographical restrictions.

Flower-Fifth Avenue Hospital
105th Street and Fifth Avenue
Dr. Ernest R. Eaton in charge.
Part pay clinic.
Geographical restrictions.

Mt. Sinai Hospital
100th Street and Fifth Avenue
Dr. Maurice Wolf in charge.
Part pay clinic.
Geographical restrictions.

St. Luke's Hospital
Amsterdam Avenue and 113th Street
Dr. John Staige Davis, Jr., in charge.
Part pay clinic.
Geographical restrictions.

Beth David Hospital
144 East 90th Street

Dr. Irving Gould in charge.
Part pay clinic.
Geographical restrictions.

Lenox Hill Hospital
76th Street and Park Avenue
Dr. Otto Steinbrocker in charge.
Part pay clinic.
Geographical restrictions.

Hospital for Special Surgery
321 East 42nd Street
Drs. Richard H. Freyberg and Cornelius H. Traeger in charge.
Part pay.
Geographical restrictions.

New York Hospital
York Avenue and 70th Street
Dr. Richard H. Freyberg in charge.
Part pay clinic.
Geographical restrictions.

City Hospital
(Welfare Island Dispensary)
80th Street and East End Avenue
Dr. Jed H. Irvine in charge.
Free clinic.
No geographical restrictions.

Metropolitan Hospital
(Welfare Island Dispensary)
80th Street and East End Avenue
Dr. Robert C. Batterman in charge.

Free clinic.
Geographical restrictions.

Roosevelt Hospital
59th Street and 9th Avenue
Dr. Cornelius Traeger in charge.
Part pay clinic.
Geographical restrictions.

St. Clare's Hospital
415 West 51st Street
Dr. William B. Rawls in charge.
Part pay clinic.
Geographical restrictions.

New York Polyclinic Hospital
345 West 50th Street
Dr. William B. Rawls in charge.
Part pay clinic.
Geographical restrictions.

French Hospital
524 West 30th Street
Dr. Emanuel Rudd in charge.
Part pay clinic.
Geographical restrictions.

Bellevue Hospital, 1st Med. Div.
Dr. Eli Bauman in charge.
Free clinic.
Geographical restrictions.

Bellevue Hospital, 2nd Med. Div.
Dr. Robert M. Lintz in charge.
Free clinic.
Geographical restrictions.

Bellevue Hospital, 3rd Med. Div.
Dr. Morris Ziff in charge.
Free clinic.
Geographical restrictions.

Bellevue Hospital, 4th Med. Div.
Dr. Edward F. Hartung in charge.
Free clinic.
Geographical restrictions.

University Hospital
303 East 20th Street
Dr. Edward F. Hartung in charge.
Part pay clinic.
Geographical restrictions.

Gouverneur Hospital
Gouverneur Square
Dr. Louis S. Ferris in charge.
Free clinic.
Geographical restrictions.

Beth Israel Hospital
Stuyvesant Square East
Dr. Jack R. Dordick in charge.
Part pay clinic.
Geographical restrictions.

New York Infirmary
321 East 15th Street
Dr. Leonora Andersen in charge.
Part pay clinic.
Geographical restrictions.

Stuyvesant Polyclinic
137 Second Avenue

MANHATTAN (continued):
Dr. Harry G. Kupperman in charge.
Part pay clinic.
No geographical restrictions.

ROCHESTER:
Rochester General Hospital
501 West Main Street
Dr. Charles LeRoy Steinberg in charge.
Free and part pay.
No geographical restrictions.

STATEN ISLAND:
St. Vincent's Hospital
Bard Avenue
Dr. Thomas T. Bowman in charge.
Part pay clinic.
Geographical restrictions.

NORTH CAROLINA
DURHAM:
*Duke Medical School

WINSTON-SALEM:
*Bowman-Gray Medical School
Wake Forest College

OHIO
AKRON:
City Hospital
525 East Market Street
Dr. Roger Q. Davis in charge.
Free clinic.
Restricted to residents of Akron and Cuyahoga Falls.

CINCINNATI:
Cincinnati General Hospital
Nathan R. Abrams, M.D., in charge.
Free clinic.
Restricted to residents of Hamilton County.

CLEVELAND:
University Hospitals of Cleveland
2065 Adelbert Road
Dr. William Clark in charge.
Part pay clinic.
Restricted to hospital's service area, unless referred by a physician.

*Lakeside Hospital
Dr. William Clark in charge.

Mt. Sinai Hospital
Dr. Ralph Wolpaw in charge.
Free and part pay.
No geographical restrictions.

City Hospital
3395 Scranton Road
Dr. Robert M. Stecher in charge.
Free and part pay.
Restricted to residents of Cleveland.

St. Luke's Hospital
11311 Shaker Boulevard
Dr. Howard H. Hopwood in charge.
Free and part pay clinic.

Restricted to residents of Cuyahoga County.

COLUMBUS:
Ohio State University Hospital
Dr. Norman O. Rothermich in
charge.
Free clinic.
No geographical restrictions.

YOUNGSTOWN:
St. Elizabeth's Hospital
1044 Belmont Avenue
Dr. M. M. Szucs in charge.
Free and part pay.
Restricted to residents of Ma-
honing, Trumbull, and Ash-
tabula counties.

OKLAHOMA

OKLAHOMA CITY:
Bone & Joint Hospital
Dr. W. K. Ishmael in charge.
Pay clinic.
No geographical restrictions.

Oklahoma State University
Hospital
Dr. W. K. Ishmael in charge.
Free clinic.
Restricted to residents of the
state of Oklahoma.

University Hospital, University
of Oklahoma
800 N.E. 13th Street
Dr. A. A. Hellbaum in charge.
Free clinic.

Restricted to indigent residents
of Oklahoma.

*Arthritis Clinic
228 N.W. 13th Street
Dr. E. Goldfain in charge.

TULSA:
Hillcrest Medical Center
1653 East 12th
Dr. S. Y. Andelman in charge.
Part pay.
No geographical restrictions.

Hillcrest Memorial Hospital
Dr. S. Y. Andelman in charge.
Part pay clinic.
Restricted to residents of north-
eastern Oklahoma.

*Tulsa County Medical Society
Welfare Building

*St. John's Hospital

OREGON

PORTLAND:
Holladay Park Clinic
1132 N.E. Second
Dr. Arthur C. Jones in charge.
Pay clinic (nominal fee).
No geographical restrictions.

University of Oregon Medical
School Hospital
3181 S.W. Marquam Hill Road
Dr. Howard P. Lewis in charge.
Free clinic.
Restricted to residents of Mult-
nomah County, but other in-

PORTLAND (continued):
digent patients taken on request.

WHEELER:
Rinehart Clinic
Dr. R. E. Rinehart in charge.
Free and part pay clinic.
No geographical restrictions.

PENNSYLVANIA

BRISTOL:
Bristol General Hospital
Wilson Avenue and Pond Street
Dr. Louis Udell in charge.
Pay clinic.
No geographical restrictions, but must be referred by physician.

BRYN MAWR:
*Bryn Mawr Hospital
Bryn Mawr Avenue
Dr. Morris A. Bowie in charge.
Free and part pay.

DANVILLE:
*The George F. Geisinger Memorial Hospital

DARBY:
Fitzgerald Mercy Hospital
Lansdowne Avenue
Drs. Patrick J. Hand and John Moran in charge.
Free and part pay clinic.
No geographical restrictions.

HARRISBURG:
Harrisburg Hospital
Dr. Nathan Sussman in charge.
Free clinic.
Restricted to residents of Cumberland, Perry, and Dauphin counties.

LANCASTER:
*Lancaster General Hospital

PHILADELPHIA:
Temple University Hospital
Dr. J. Lansbury in charge.
Part pay clinic.
No geographical restrictions.

Hahnemann Medical College Hospital
230 N. Broad Street
Dr. H. E. Banghart in charge.
Free and part pay clinic.
No geographical restrictions.

Albert Einstein Medical Center (South Division)
5th and Reed Street
Dr. Irvin F. Hermann.
Free clinic.
No geographical restrictions.

Pennsylvania Hospital
8th and Spruce Streets
Dr. Richard T. Smith in charge.
Free and part pay.
No geographical restrictions.

Jefferson Medical College Hospital

10th and Walnut Streets
Dr. Richard T. Smith in
charge.
Free and part pay.
No geographical restrictions.

Jefferson Hospital
10th and Walnut Streets
Dr. Irvin F. Hermann.
Part pay clinic.
No geographical restrictions.

Presbyterian Hospital
51 North 39th Street
Dr. George F. Cormeny in
charge.
Free and part pay.
No geographical restrictions.

Philadelphia General Hospital
34th and Curie Avenue
Dr. Abraham Cohen in charge.
Free and part pay.
Restricted to residents of Phila-
delphia area.

Hospital of the University of
Pennsylvania
3400 Spruce Street
Dr. Joseph L. Hollander in
charge.
Free and part pay clinic.
No geographical restrictions.

*Children's Hospital
1740 Bainbridge Street
Dr. Rachel Ash in charge.
Free and part pay.

*Germantown Hospital
600 E. Wister Street

Dr. Corson White in charge.
Free and part pay clinic.

*Jewish Hospital
York Road and Olney Avenue
Dr. A. Rosenfeld.
Free and part pay clinic.

*Mercy-Douglass Hospital
50th and Woodland Avenue
Dr. Edward E. Hollaway in
charge.
Free and part pay.

*Mt. Sinai Hospital
1429 S. 5th Street
Dr. A. Rubenstone in charge.
Part pay clinic.

*Women's Hospital
Preston and Parrish Streets
Dr. Juliet Nathanson in charge.
Free and part pay clinic.

*Abington Memorial Hospital

*Graduate Hospital

PITTSBURGH:
*Allegheny General Hospital
320 E. North Avenue
Dr. Paul B. Steele in charge.

Montefiore Hospital
3459 Fifth Avenue
Dr. H. M. Margolis in charge.
Free and part pay clinic.
Restricted to residents of Alle-
gheny County.

Shadyside Hospital
5230 Center Avenue

PITTSBURGH (continued):
Dr. William B. Spinelli in charge.
Free clinic.
No geographical restrictions.

Falk Clinic
University of Pittsburgh
3601 Fifth Avenue
Dr. H. M. Margolis in charge.
Free and part pay.
No geographical restrictions.

St. Margaret Memorial Hospital
265 — 46th Street
Dr. H. M. Margolis in charge.
Free and part pay clinic.
Restricted to residents of Allegheny County.

WILKES-BARRE:
Laurel Hospital
Laurel Run
Dr. Nicholas Mauriello in charge.
Private clinic.
No geographical restrictions.
(Physical Medicine Rehabilitation Service.)

RHODE ISLAND
PROVIDENCE:
St. Joseph's Hospital
Broad and Peace Streets
Dr. William J. O'Connell in charge.
Free and part pay.
No geographical restrictions.

TENNESSEE
MEMPHIS:
Campbell Clinic, Incorporated
869 Madison Avenue
10 member partnership clinic.
Full pay.
No geographical restrictions.

TEXAS
DALLAS:
*Southwestern Medical School
University of Texas

*Parkland Hospital
Oak Lawn and Maple Avenue

Texas Scottish Rite Hospital
2201 Welborn
Dr. Brandon Carrell in charge.
Free clinic.
Admits only children from the state of Texas.

W. B. Carroll Clinic
3701 Maple Avenue
Dr. Howard C. Coggeshall in charge.

HOUSTON:
Southern Pacific Hospital
2015 Thomas
Dr. M. D. Levy in charge.
For railroad employees only.

MARLIN:
The Buie Clinic and Buie-Allen Hospital

229 Coleman Street
Dr. Neil D. Buie in charge.
Part pay clinic.
No geographical restrictions.

Torbett Clinic and Hospital
401 Coleman Street
Dr. J. B. Barnett in charge.
Pay clinic.
No geographical restrictions.

*Clinic in Mineral Wells

SAN ANTONIO:
*Robert B. Green Memorial
   Hospital
515 Morales Street

VERMONT

BURLINGTON:
Mary Fletcher Hospital
Dr. John H. Bland in charge.
Free and part pay clinic.
No geographical restrictions.

VIRGINIA

Medical College of Virginia
   Hospital
1200 E. Broad Street
Dr. Elam C. Toone, Jr., in
   charge.
Free and part pay clinic.
No geographical restrictions.

WASHINGTON

SEATTLE:
King County Hospital
Department of Medicine
University of Washington
325 Ninth Avenue
Free clinic.
Restricted to residents of King
   County, unless special re-
   ferral is made.

*Harborview County Hospital

WISCONSIN

MADISON:
University Hospitals
The University of Wisconsin
1300 University Avenue
Dr. William P. Deiss in charge.
Part-pay clinic.
No geographical restrictions—
   referral by physician.

MILWAUKEE:
Milwaukee County Dispensary
Dr. Mark W. Garry in charge.
Free clinic.
Restricted to indigent residents
   of Milwaukee County.

WOOD:
Veterans Administration Hos-
   pital
Dr. Mark W. Garry in charge.
Restricted to veterans of Wis-
   consin.

INDEX